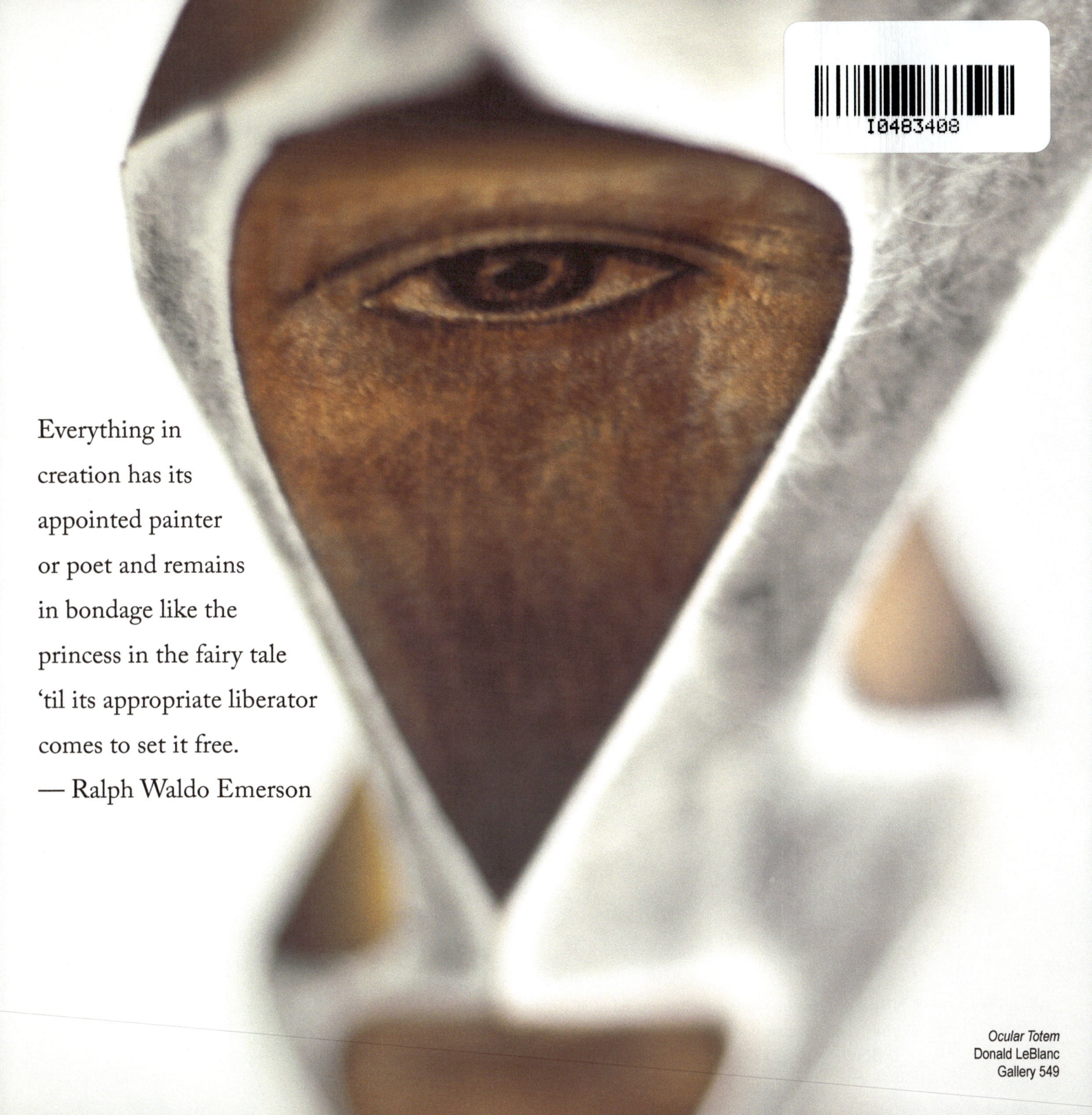

Everything in creation has its appointed painter or poet and remains in bondage like the princess in the fairy tale 'til its appropriate liberator comes to set it free.
— Ralph Waldo Emerson

Ocular Totem
Donald LeBlanc
Gallery 549

THE ACADIANA ART✦TRAIL

THE ESSENTIAL GUIDE TO FINDING LOCAL ART IN CAJUN COUNTRY.

BY KELLI FORET
PHOTOS BY LAUREN HENSGENS

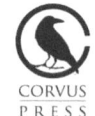

CORVUS
PRESS

ISBN 978-0-9829239-5-5 Contact Corvus Press for Library of Congress catalog information.

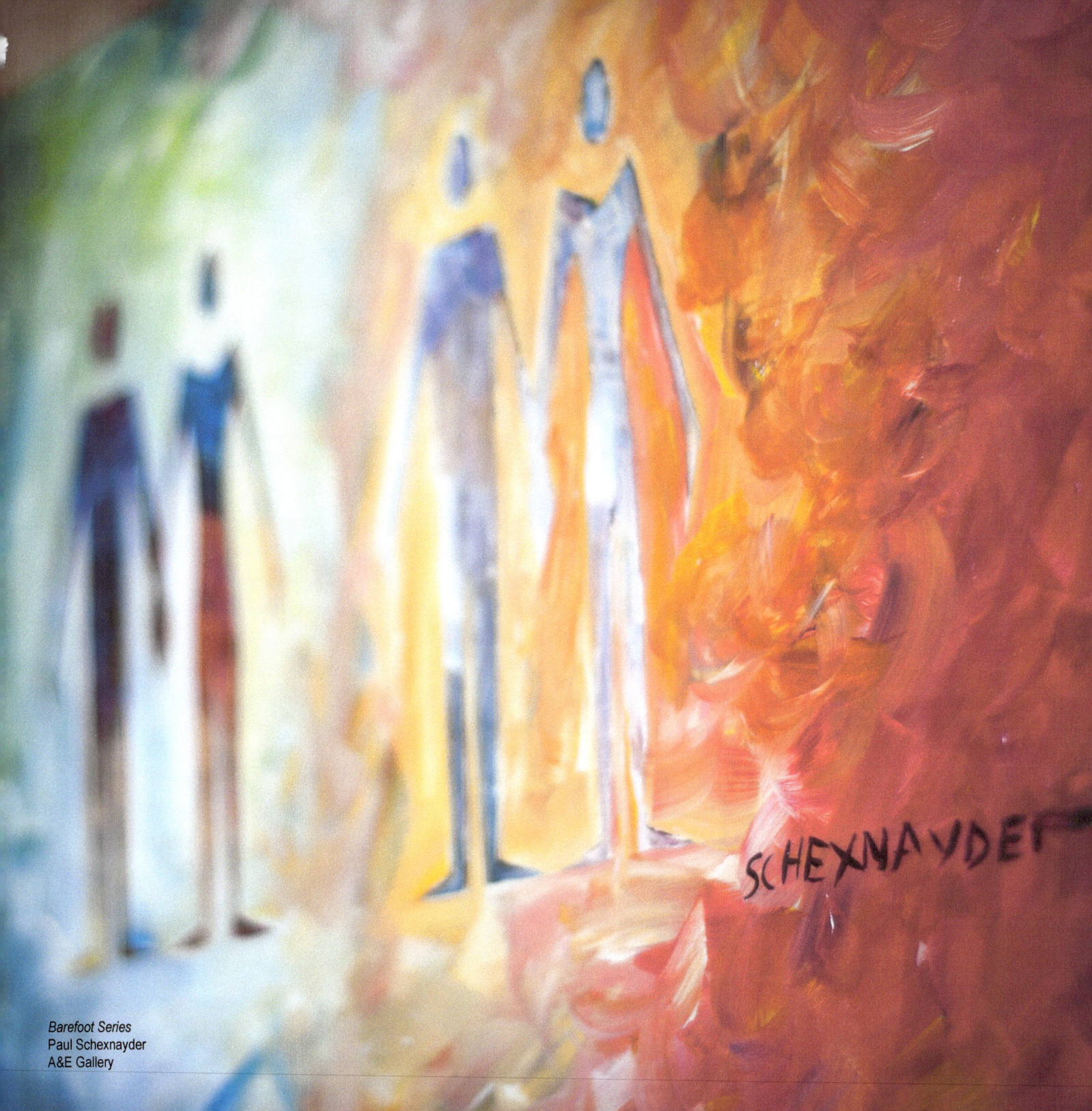

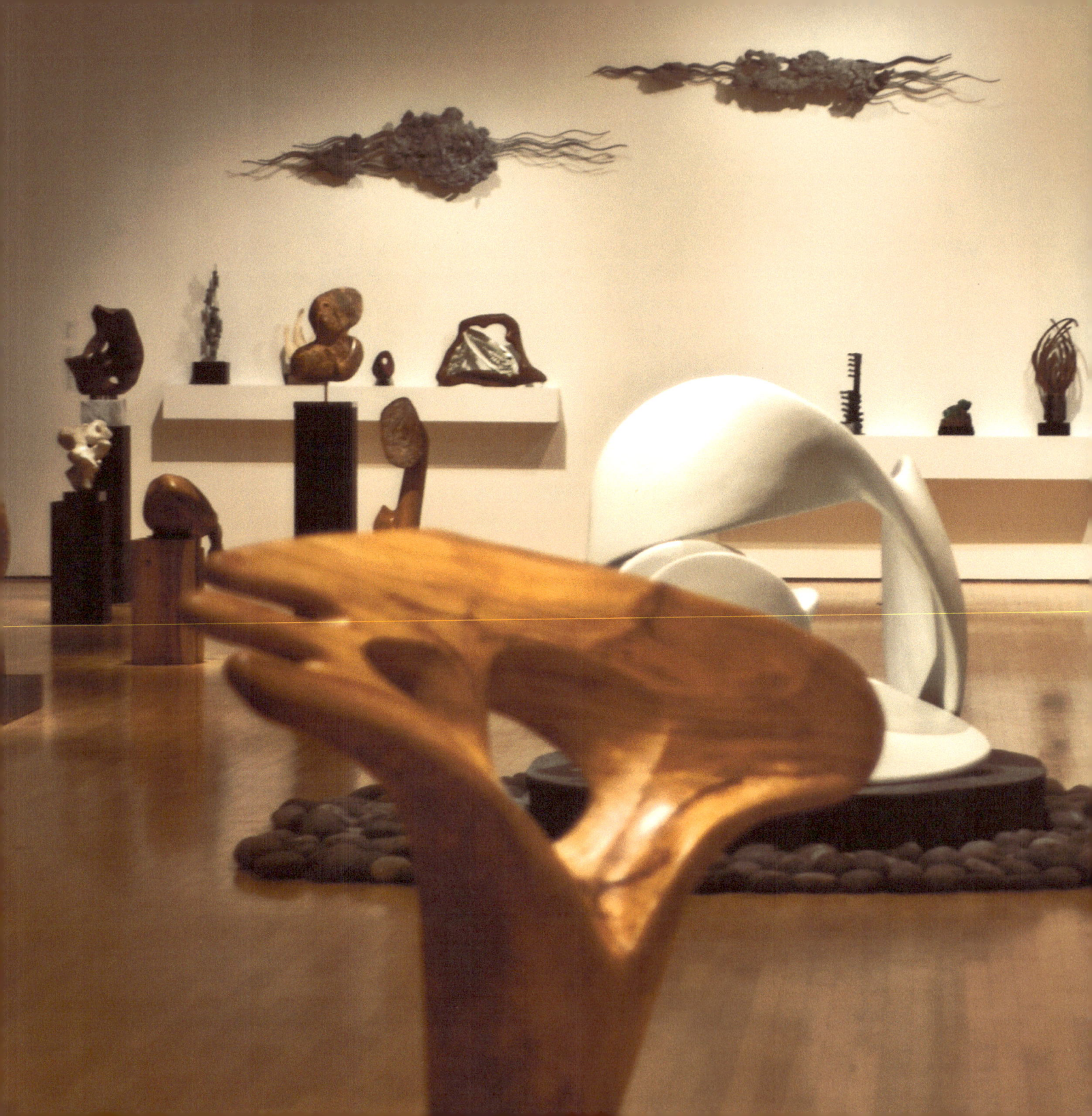

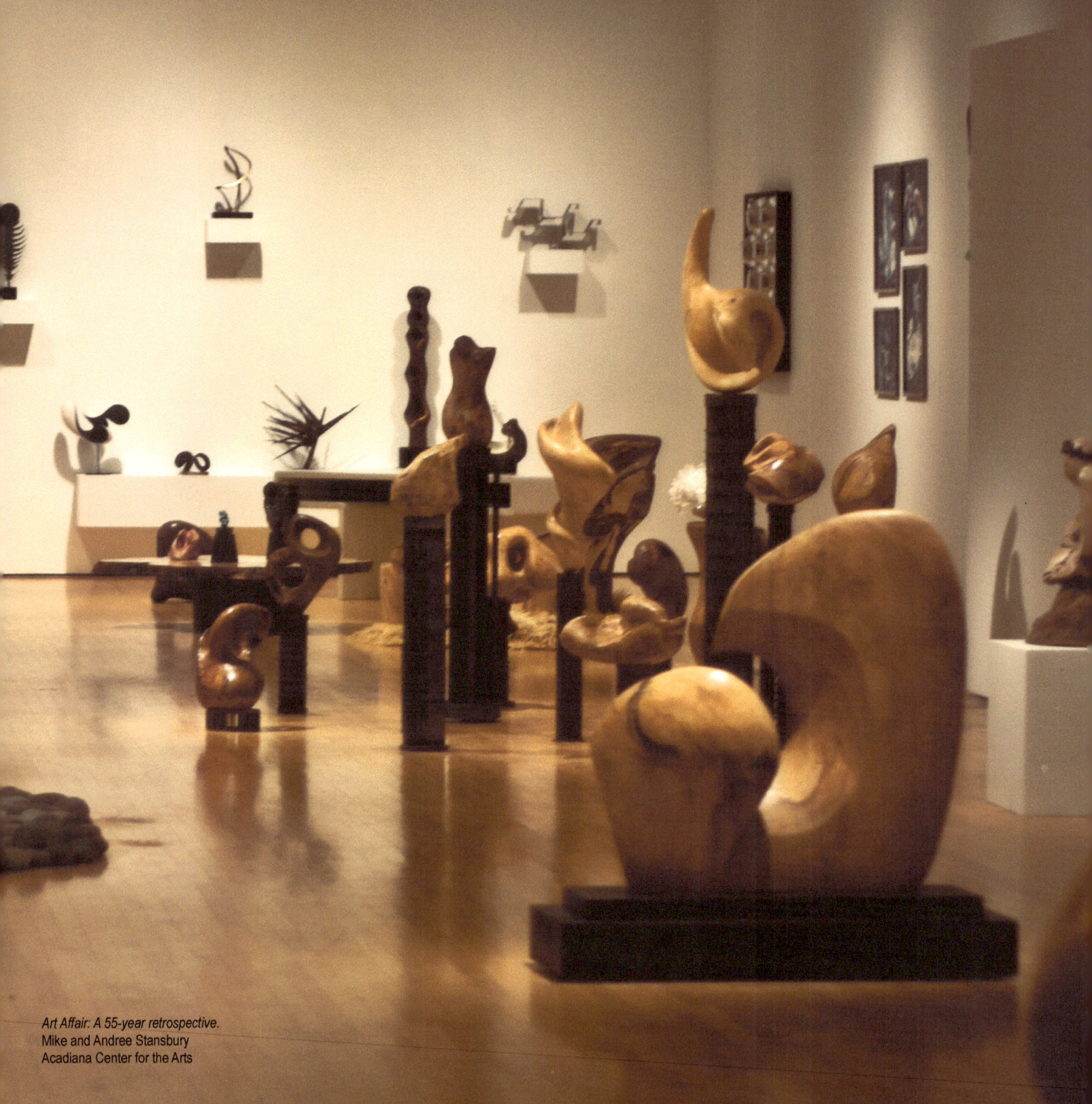

Art Affair: A 55-year retrospective.
Mike and Andree Stansbury
Acadiana Center for the Arts

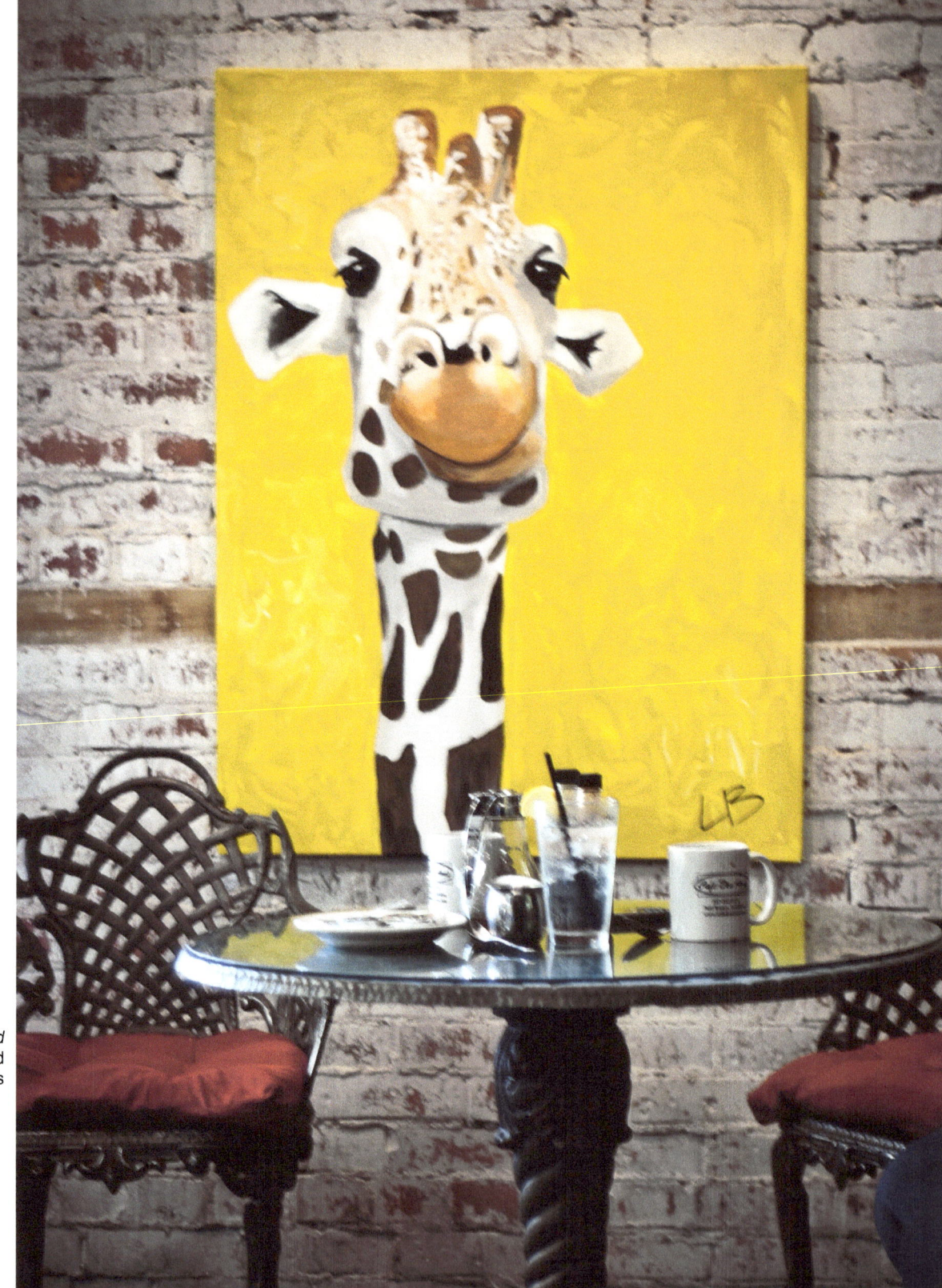

Floyd
Logan Berard
Café Des Amis

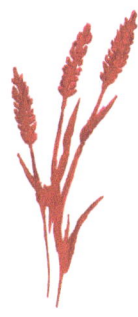

For Mom, Dad, Chris, Del and Troy ... thanks for your love and support;
and for Lola, Evie and Caroline ... my little art trailers.

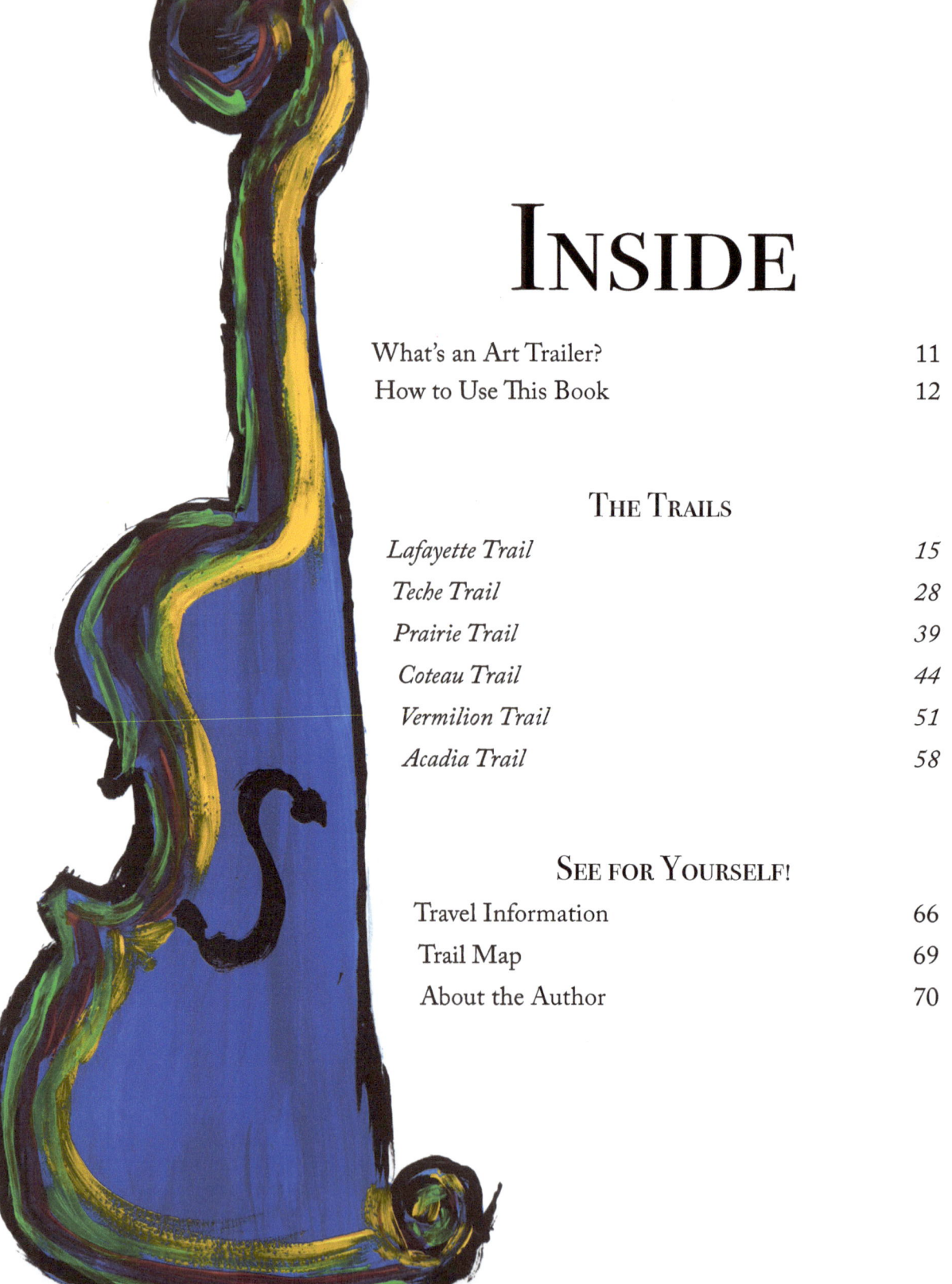

INSIDE

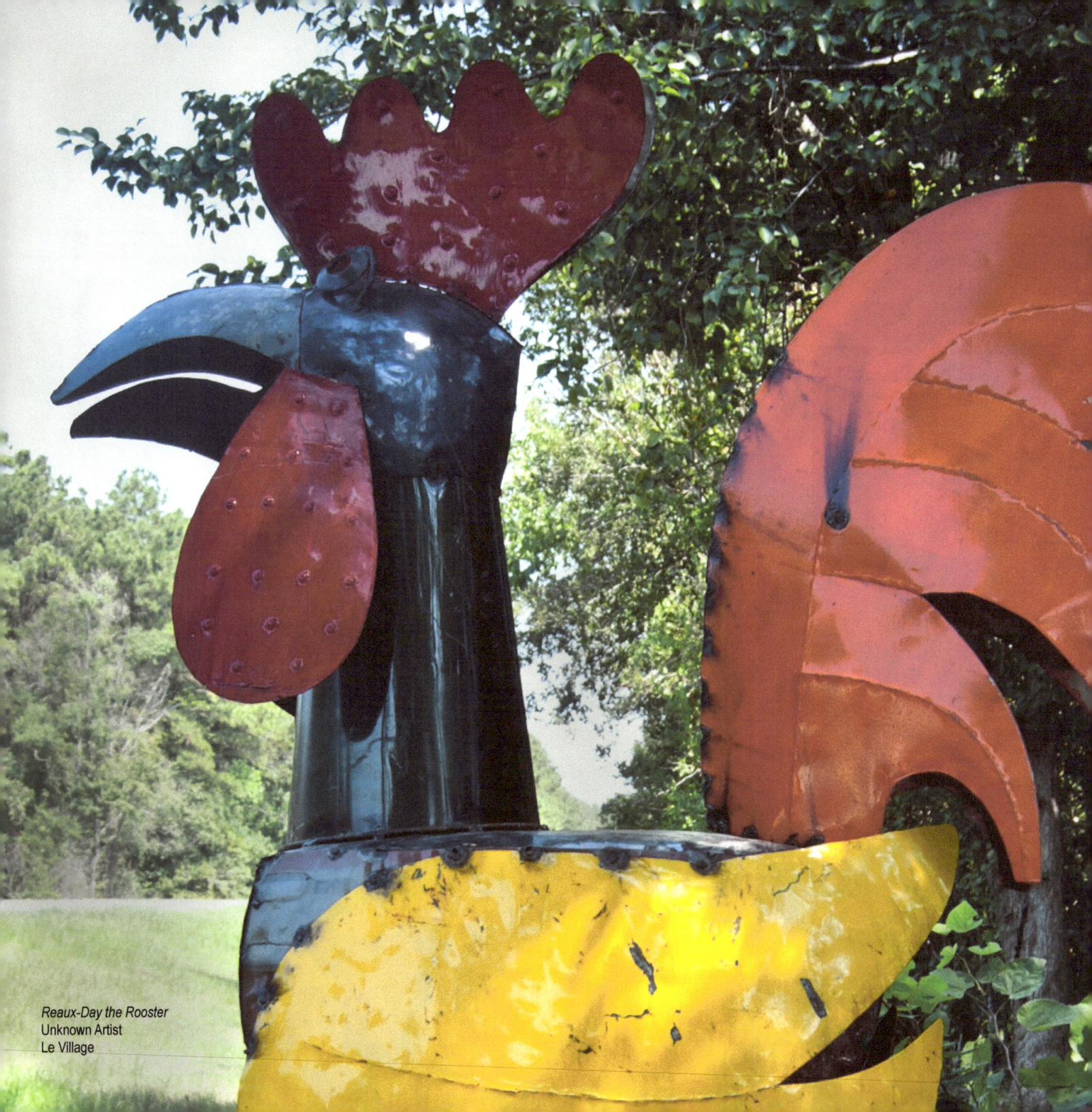

Reaux-Day the Rooster
Unknown Artist
Le Village

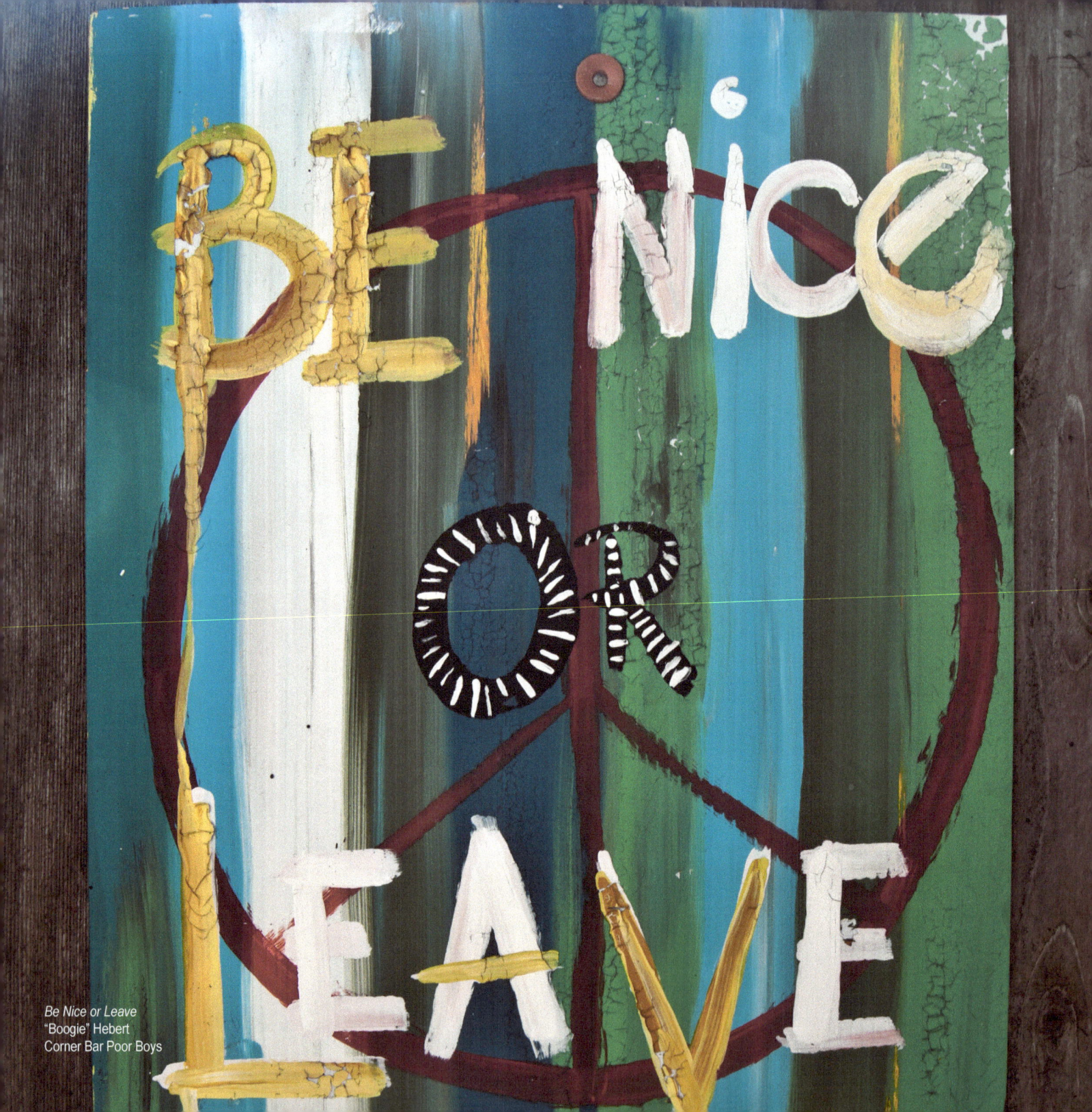

Be Nice or Leave
"Boogie" Hebert
Corner Bar Poor Boys

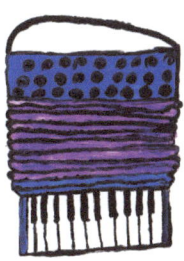

Art Trailer: |ärt trāler|

1. n. A mobile home with art in it.

2. n. A fan of locally-produced art who is unafraid to take dirt roads, back alleys and adventurous paths to the most unique, sometimes unheard-of galleries.

For me, part of the fun of art is the treasure hunt. It's about digging into the small-small town discussion. It's about getting off the beaten path. It's about finding your way to the most fun, unique, obscure and must-see venues to purchase and enjoy art.

I love adventure. If that adventure involves art — even new things I never-before considered to be art — I love it more. This often leads me to museums, galleries, private showings, studios, cafés, restaurants, barns, homes and more. That's what I call art-adventure.

I love the headline spaces as much as the ones that aren't considered "mainstream" galleries. In fact, many aren't galleries at all, but coffee shops and local markets — places that an authentic, budding, perhaps struggling artist might be grateful to display their work. They are sometimes not what's considered "exclusive" showrooms, but instead venues that house the most unique and obscure expressions, gritty and undiscovered. I have an undying urge to discover the galleries you won't find in most tour guides, city maps and travel bulletins. It's a disease … but it's definitely not a curse.

This book is the result of being unafraid to knock on a door to tour a private gallery, drive through a field to get to golden eggs (literally) and explore old buildings that have now become a studio. It's an effort to make it easier for you to uncover the most unique artistic treasures this incredible area we call Acadiana has to offer … you're in for a treat.

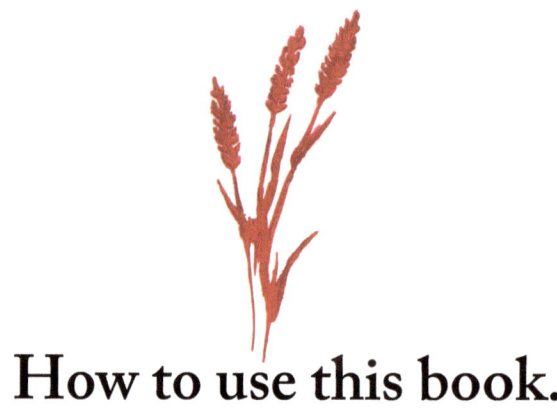

How to use this book.

This book is divided into six trails — or day trips — so you can explore these hidden gems in easy fashion. For the most part, one full day is required for each trail.

Each trail includes a map that starts in Acadiana's hub city of Lafayette. In Lafayette you'll find a full compliment of hotels, a growing airport and some of the most incredible food around (it's been recognized nationally for its good restaurants, but that's another book). The gallery owners are extremely welcoming and happy to help direct you to the next venue.

Wednesday through Saturday seems to be the best time to visit venues as most are closed Sunday through Tuesday. Some studios/venues that may require a phone call or a little pre-planning and you'll see where I've pointed those out.

If you're feeling social, take a few friends or (if you're like me) go it alone for some much needed self-reflection time. These trails make great romantic dates, fun birthday parties, learning opportunities for kids and they fuel conversation in group gatherings. It's inexpensive, educational, intriguing and fun. Take a drive. What do you have to lose?

We want to hear what you think: Upon visiting a venue, ask them to sign the header page of each trail. Once you've completed a trail, tell us about it at ArtTrailLady.com. We'll post your photo and comments about that particular trail. Once you've completed the *entire* Acadiana Art Trail, we'll post your name on our wall of fame with your personal comments on Acadiana's local art scene. Your feedback will continue to help us shape updates on the book and help others discover the best of what's hidden in local art.

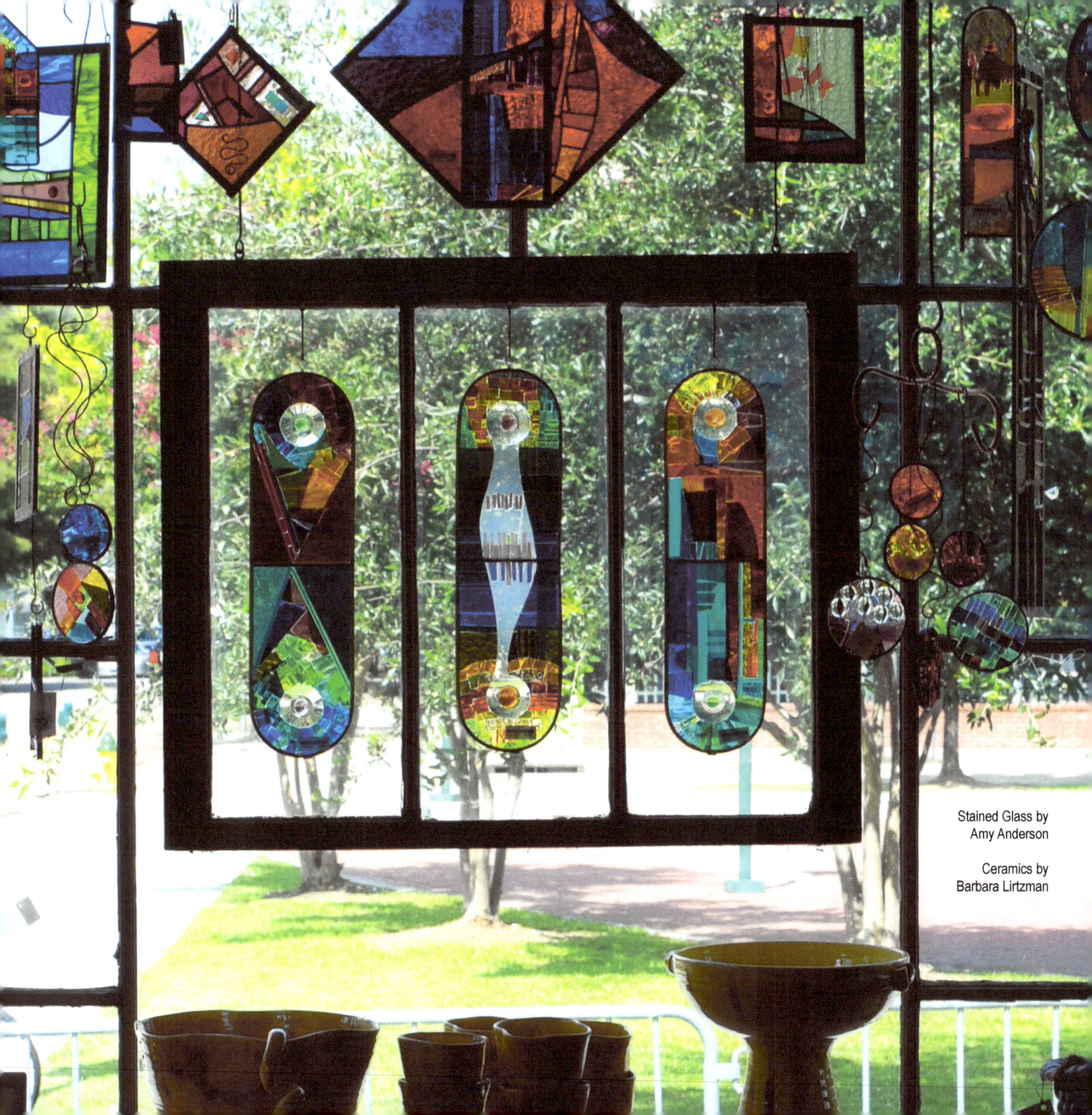

Stained Glass by
Amy Anderson

Ceramics by
Barbara Lirtzman

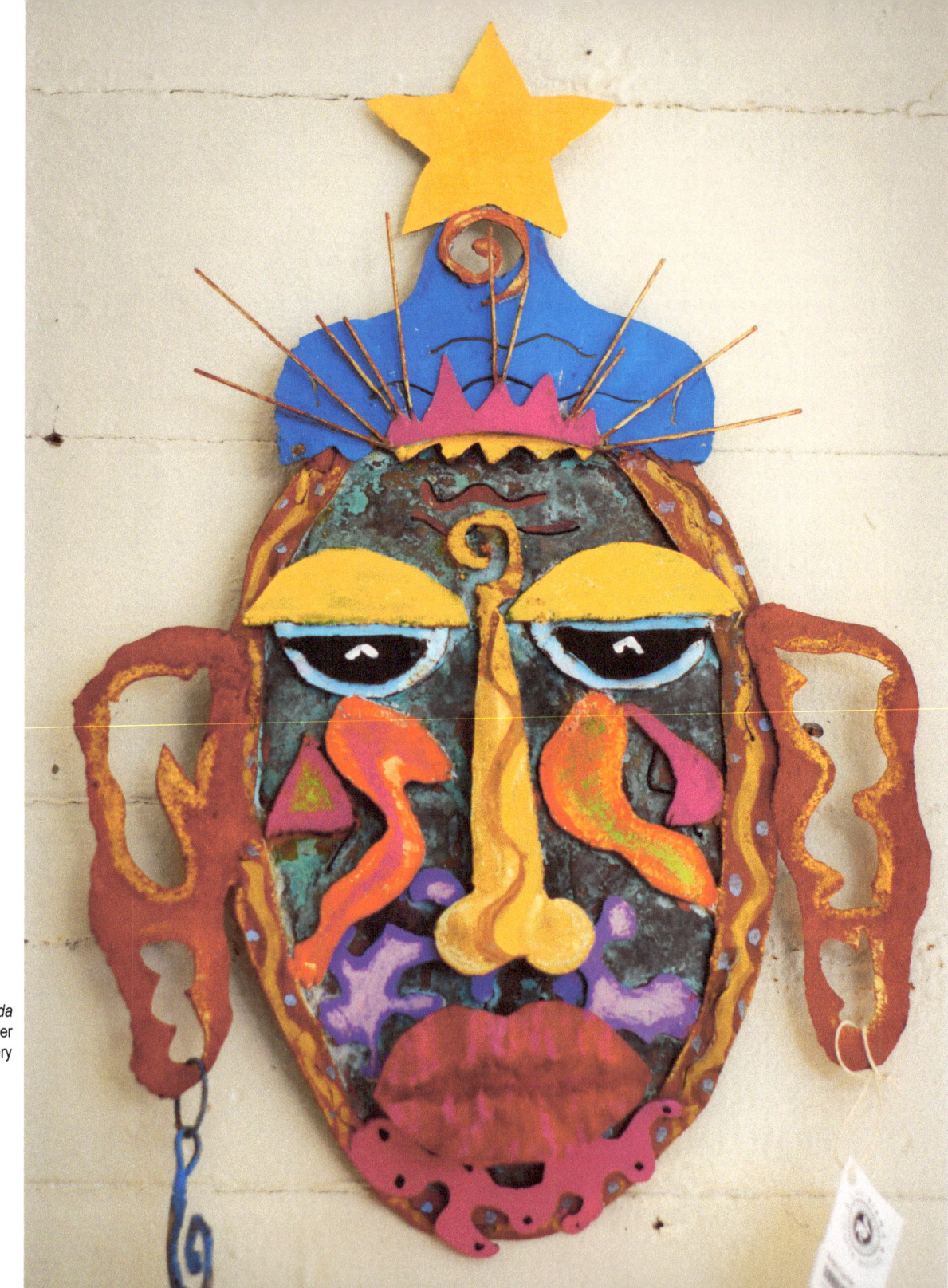

Bhudda
Susan Carver
San Souci Gallery

14

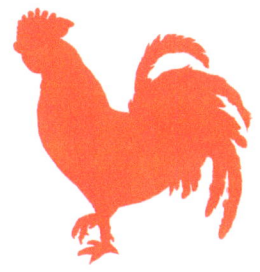

Lafayette Trail

There's a famous Cajun song called "Allons à Lafayette" ("Let's go to Lafayette") recorded by Joe Falcon and Cléoma Breaux in 1928. It describes Lafayette as a hub city, a center point for culture and commerce. You'll still here locals repeat the chorus as they make their way to the hub city for dancing, eating, shopping and of course arts and culture. Fittingly, that's where the first art trail begins.

Trail Lafayette makes for a full day, so get an early start if one day is all you have. The best time to journey the Lafayette Trail is during Second Saturday ArtWalk, a downtown Lafayette tradition. Galleries open early and stay open late for the monthly event, often opening new showings and offering food and wine. That said, just about any Wednesday through Saturday are good days to Trail Lafayette as well.

AMERICA'S COFFEE HOUSE
403-B South Buchanan Street — Lafayette

With dreams of having a creative space for artisans to collaborate, Floyd Willis combined coffee with the local downtown vibe and Americas Coffee House was born. Local artists and creatives collaborate here often. The atmosphere is unique, exquisite, and chic. "I feel smarter when I'm here … I feel productive," says regular, Kay Couvillon.

Here you'll find work from photographers like Floyd Willis, Glen Clark, Chris Deville and painter, Chootie Von Ghoul. Their pieces line the white warehouse walls of the shop. Don't miss the cup art. Regulars contribute to the atmosphere by painting, writing and drawing on Americas' coffee cups which are displayed throughout the shop. Exploring Americas is a must if you find yourself in downtown Lafayette.

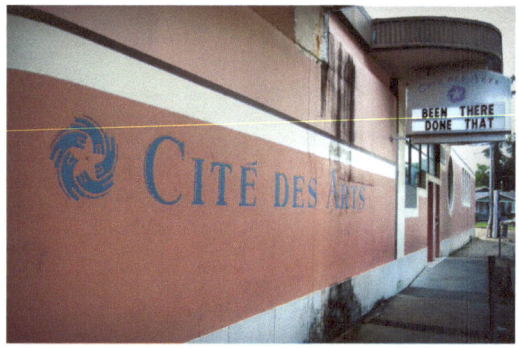

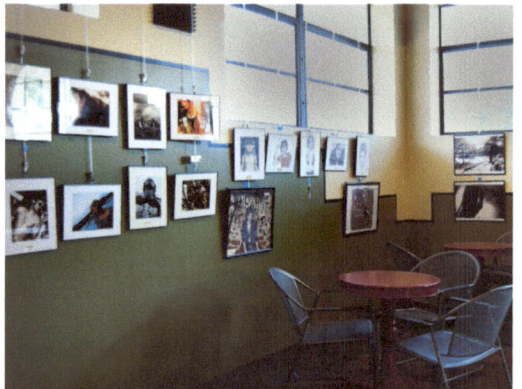

CITÉ DES ARTS
109 Vine Street — Lafayette

Theater spaces, café, dance, art gallery, rental space, music, drama, film, poetry — it's pretty rare to find each of these genres in a single site. "A grass roots community arts center where cultures connect," is how Cite des Arts describes itself. The 109 Vine St. building contains all you've come for. Stop in for a quick review of the quirky visual art but plan in advance for an original, indie play or music series, as many sell out.

Left: Cité des Arts hosts an eclectic mix of art, from modern photography to independent, locally-produced plays.

Right: America's has become a Lafayette creative hub where you'll often find creative professionals discussing projects in its museum-like atmosphere.

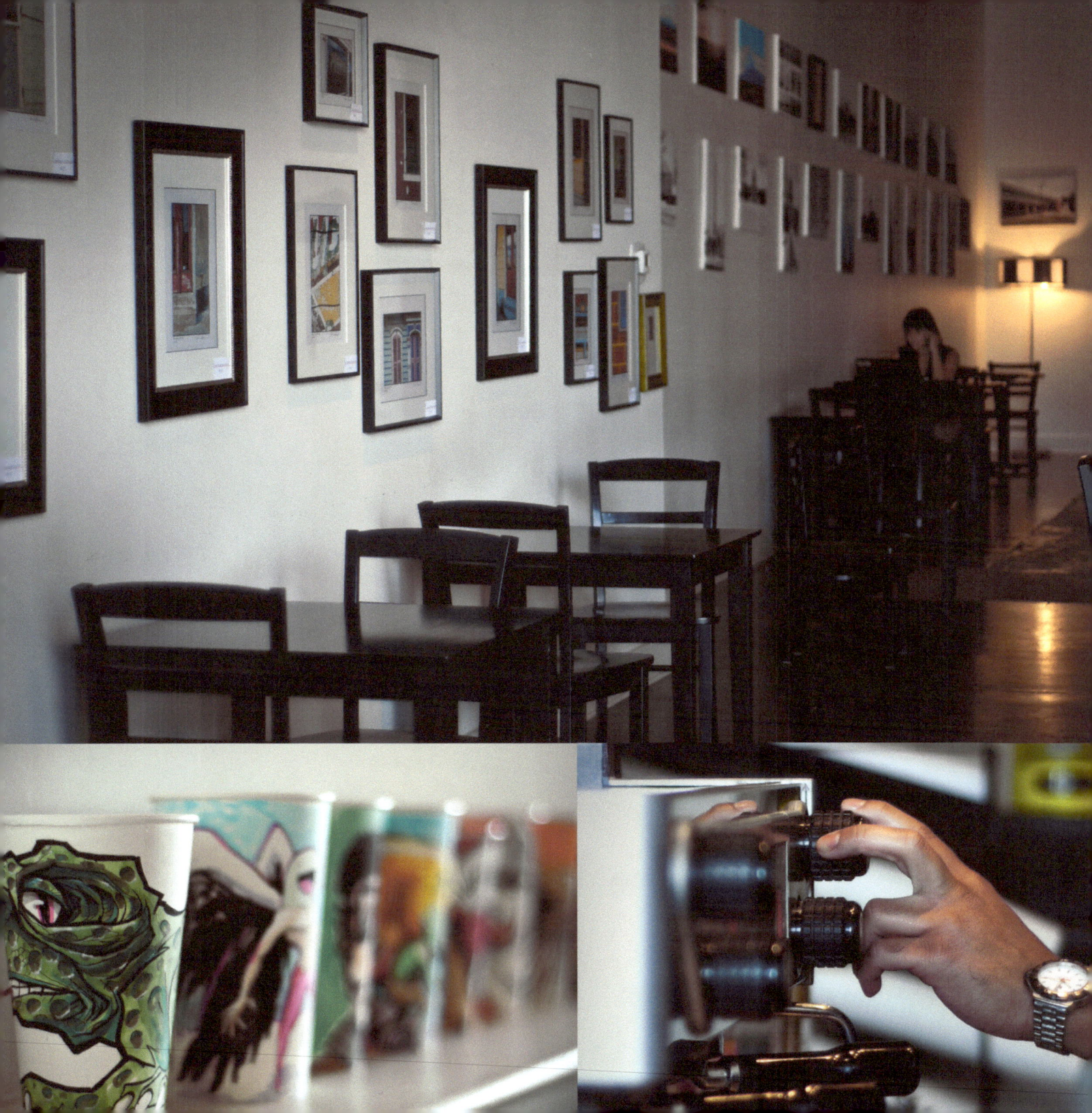

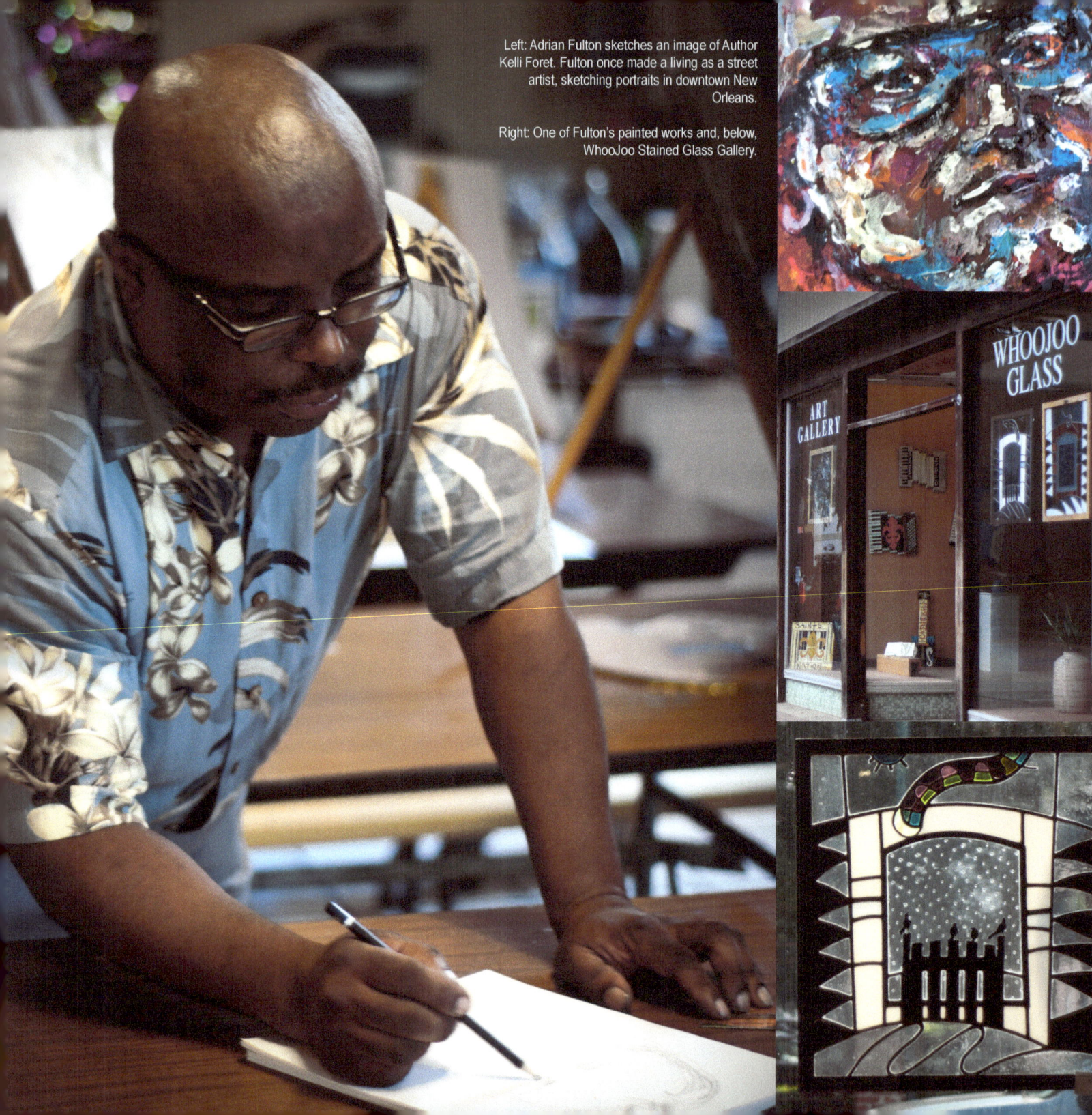

Left: Adrian Fulton sketches an image of Author Kelli Foret. Fulton once made a living as a street artist, sketching portraits in downtown New Orleans.

Right: One of Fulton's painted works and, below, WhooJoo Stained Glass Gallery.

ADRIAN FULTON'S FINE ART GALLERY

302 Jefferson Street — Lafayette

Brace yourself, but Fulton's use of texture, color and imagination will blow your mind! Known for portraits of well-known people from around the world like Mother Theresa, Michael Jackson and Bruce Lee, his purely remarkable talent attracted Mrs. Laura Bush so much, he was invited to the White House in December 2008. This gallery features not only the work of Fulton but also those who study with him through art classes and therapy. Fulton often paints during electrical storms, saying it adds energy to his work. This "hidden" gallery is one of the area's best.

INSIDER'S TIP

If you're timing's right, Adrian might sketch one of his famous 10-minute portraits of you.

WhooJoo Stained Glass Gallery

532 Jefferson Street — Lafayette

As I followed the vintage mosaic tile leading into the heart of this glass gallery, I couldn't help but to think of Tennessee William's *The Glass Menagerie*. You'll love exploring each glass masterpiece, including welded works encasing a spectrum of colors and rainbow beams of light showing through the heart of oak branches.

Shop Owner Craig McCullen greeted me with open arms and a smile. Originating as a stain glass shop thirty years ago, WhooJoo Stained Glass Gallery, metamorphosed into an art gallery focused on McCullen's stained glass masterpieces. The gallery showcases work of other local favorites — Mike Stansbury, David Alpha, Tanya Schulze, Neil Nehrbass and my favorite, McCullen's daughter, Claire McCullen and her origami.

McCullen's work not only spotlights his free, impressionist styled pieces but also includes refurbished stained glass windows from historic churches in the area and commissioned pieces for homes and buildings. It's completely different, a mosaic menagerie of wonder.

INSIDER'S TIP

WhooJoo Stained Glass Gallery is usually closed Saturdays except for Lafayette's Downtown Development Authority's "Second Saturday ArtWalk" celebrations, the second Saturday of each month.

GALLERY 549

549 Jefferson Street — Lafayette

For the last twelve years, Gallery 549 and its owner, Donald Leblanc, have been at the core of helping to create what is now the "downtown art scene" in Lafayette. Gallery 549 features LeBlanc's work and that of local favorites like Frederic O. Daspit. In addition, this gallery usually showcases a gumbo of styles, catering to all different taste among Lafayette locals.

LeBlanc's love for organizing art exhibitions becomes apparent when discussing important venues for local artists. When conversing with locals on their favorite gallery hot spots, Gallery 549 always tops the list. Have a quiet conversation with Donald and get insight into the latest masterpieces downtown Lafayette has to offer.

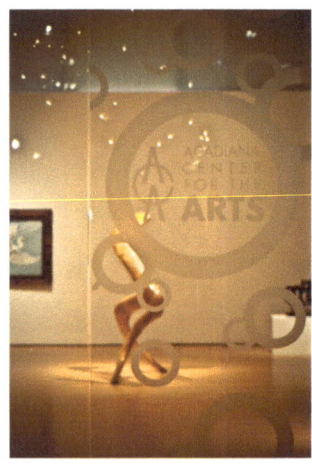

Above: ACA boasts extensive gallery space plus a 300-seat theater for live events.

Right: Donald LeBlanc experiments with a variety of textures and methods. This color-pencil work consists of roughly 50 pieces.

ACADIANA CENTER FOR THE ARTS

101 West Vermilion Street — Lafayette

Acadiana Center for the Arts (ACA) is difficult to miss. The beautifully reconstructed building on the corner of Jefferson and Vermilion Street showcases a sprawling galleries of local and national talent. ACA's swanky, smart feel gives way to the excellence of the community development, education, performances and exhibits.

I like to make my stops there during Second Saturday ArtWalk. It blends luxury with reveling in the modern folk art, especially local favorite Paul Schexnayder. With three galleries to choose from, performing arts on the second floor and surrounded by Lafayette's downtown nightlife, ACA makes a great choice for nighttime fun.

INSIDER'S TIP

ACA always does an impeccable job of choosing expressive, contemplative pieces that employ your mind to focus on thought and feeling. So, if this is your thing, ACA is the place to find it!

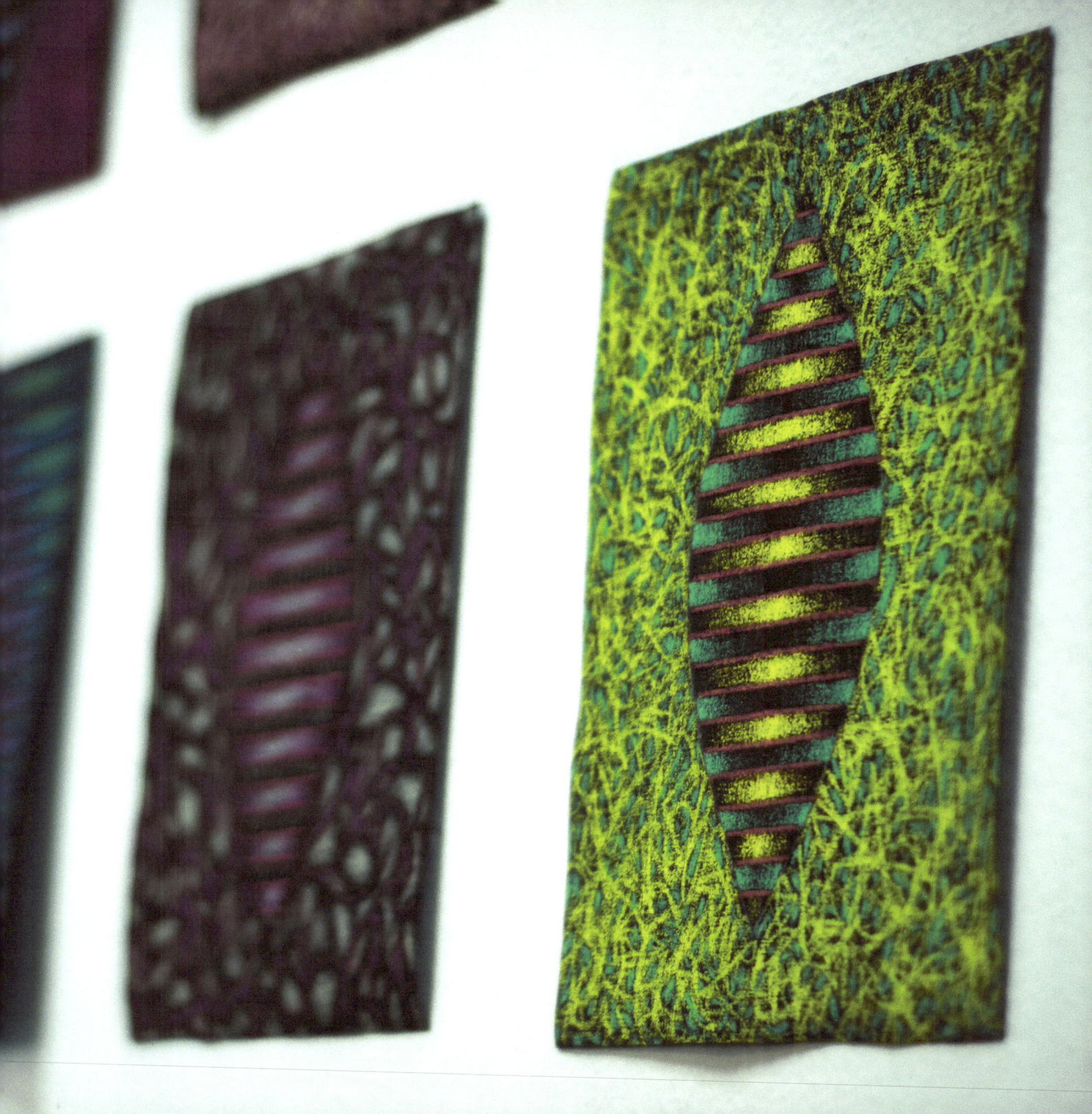

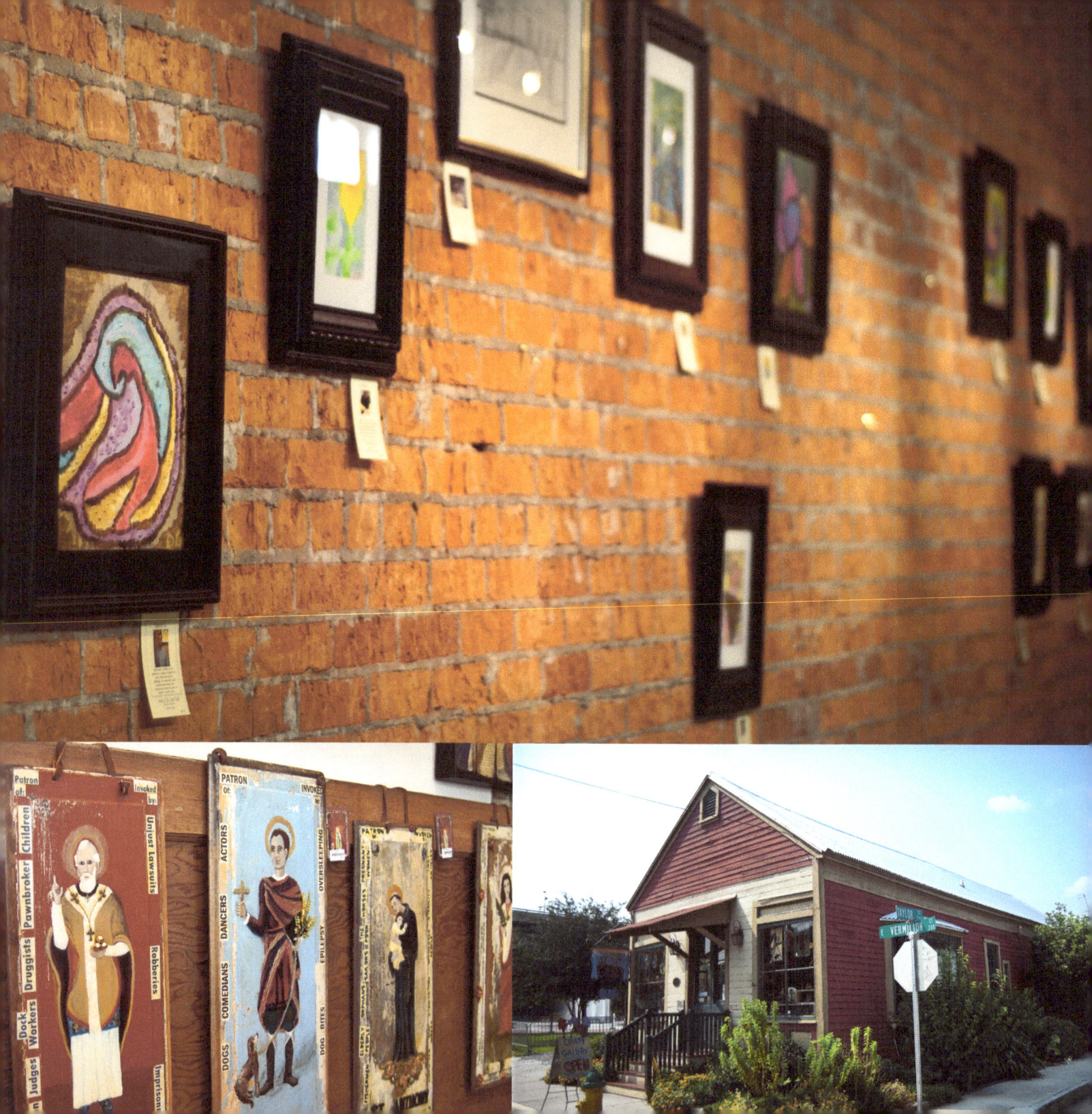

ST. PIERRE'S CENTER FOR THE ARTS

118 West Vermilion Street — Lafayette

Truly one of Lafayette's awe-striking art treasures, St. Pierre's Center for the Arts specializes in art therapy for those with disabilities. Artists here are taught how to express themselves through painting and other forms of visual arts. The studio transforms into a city-style art gallery for events like Second Saturday ArtWalk. Artists' mesmerizing works are for sale and proceeds go back to artists for supplies, and more. This is where the paintbrush creates meditative healing and you'll feel it in their sometimes scribbled masterpieces.

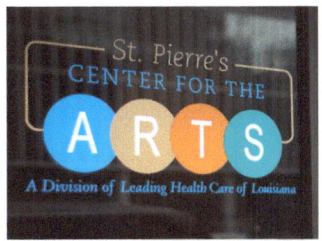

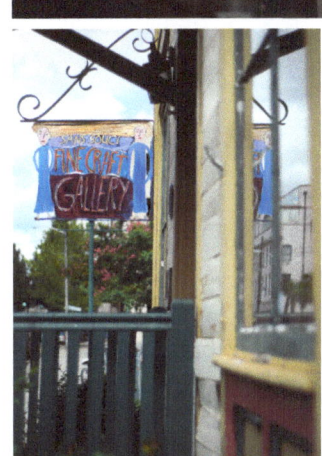

Above: You'll find St. Pierre's, San Souci and several other galleries conveniently located in Lafayette's downtown.

Left Top: Artists at St. Pierre's put on an impressive display at each Second Saturday ArtWalk.

Left Bottom: San Souci boasts art and crafts in a variety of media, including these popular modern renditions of classic religious icons by Sher Chappell.

THE SAN SOUCI GALLERY

219 East Vermilion Street — Lafayette

Home to the Louisiana Crafts Guild, Sans Souci should be a stop on every art trailer's list. Branch out from traditional painting and absorb the gallery's craft focus.

The historic building houses work of functional art pieces from known artists such as Susan Carter, Suzanne and David Wortman, Bruce Gauthier, Shine and Willie Sonnier and more. The works are indigenous to our area and are often constructed from objects found in Louisiana culture, wildlife and scenery. In order to showcase work here, artists' materials must be completely original and handmade.

Be sure to ask about the History of Sans Souci book made for shop goers to enjoy. The building is practically a work of art and certainly tells its own story. You'll quickly find why Southern Living and Traveler's Magazine call Sans Souci a must-see.

RODRIGUE STUDIO

1434 S. College Road — Lafayette

You may never expect to be greeted with a smile and very warm welcome at a world-renowned gallery, but that's what happens here. My attitude of "if you've seen one blue dog, you've seen them all" was quickly dismissed as I was continuously impressed by Rodrigue's talent and range of styles throughout the gallery. There's an air to the gallery that's uplifting.

Why had I not come to a place that was right under my nose? Perhaps I let my preconceived notions get the better or me. This a perfect stop for art trailers looking for a renewed sense of energy. The friendly, small, personal feel of the space is a treasure.

LAFAYETTE ART ASSOCIATION & GALLERY

1008 East St. Mary Boulevard — Lafayette

"Established in 1959 by artists and art connoisseurs to promote, support, encourage, and educate in the visual arts," Lafayette Art Association and Gallery ranks as one of my favorite stops on Trail Lafayette. I'm a sucker for downtowns and that's where I hunt first for galleries, so almost missed this Oil Center gem.

Right away, local favorite Hope Hebert's abstract pieces welcomed me into the gallery and prepared me for the creative explosion ahead. Feminine chatter commonly fills the back rooms and you'll often hear passionate conversations about watercolor and other techniques.

You'll easily comb the gallery uninterrupted as the staff there understands the need to explore the vibrant pieces. Sketches, pottery, photography, jewelry and sculpture stand proud against neutral grey walls making it easy to appreciate the decadent artwork.

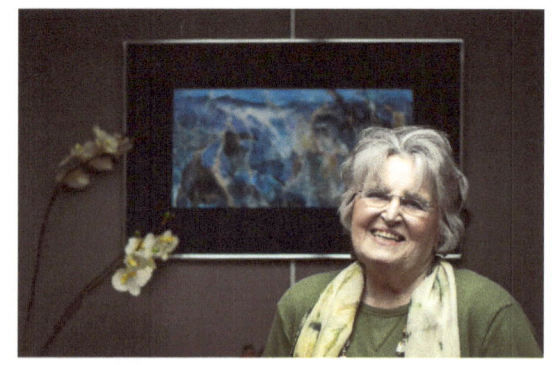

Above: Sarah Parker is both accomplished artist and director of the Lafayette Art Association.

Right: The collection at Lafayette Art Association's gallery continues to shift, offering you an ongoing reason to return.

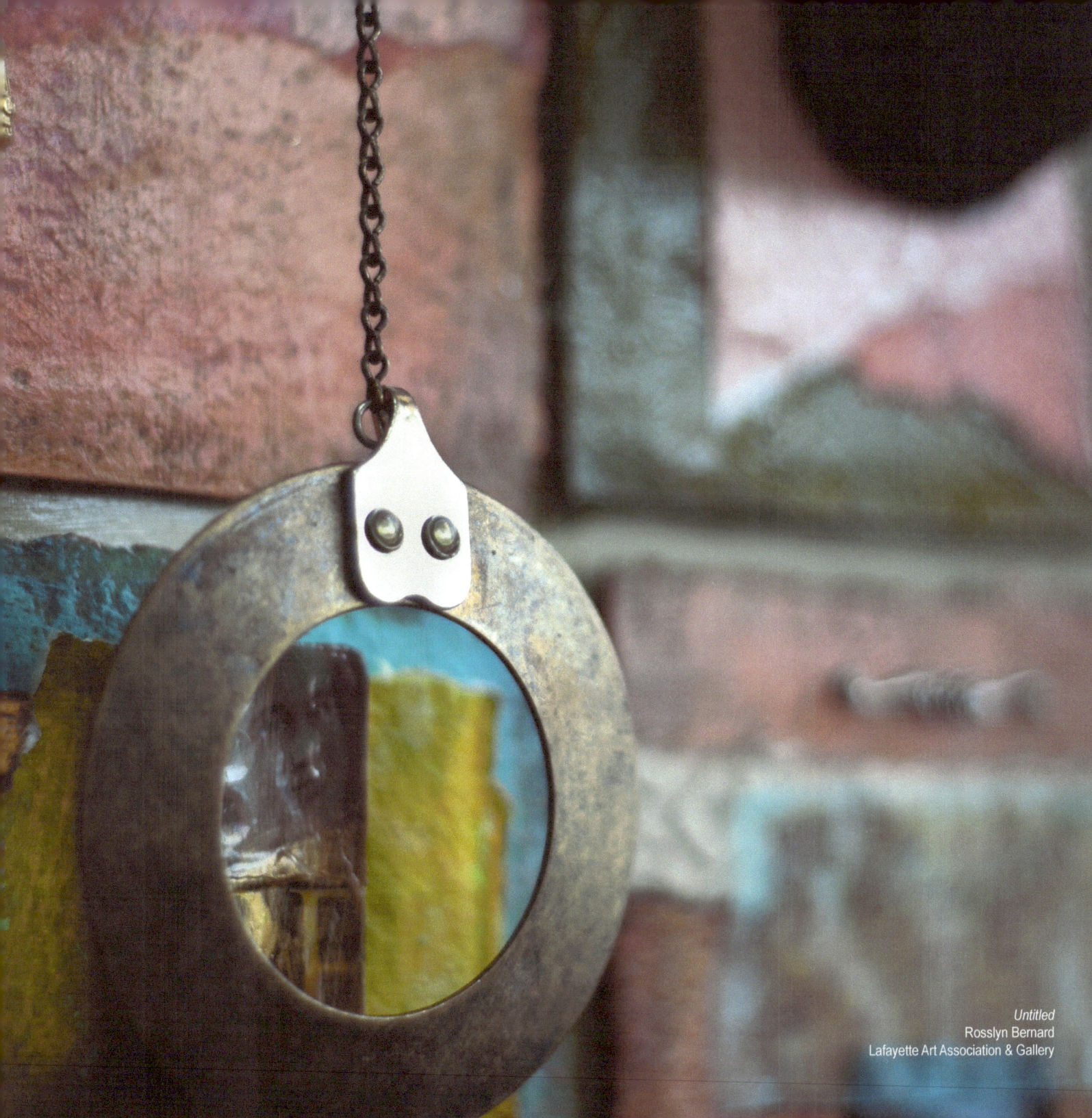

Untitled
Rosslyn Bernard
Lafayette Art Association & Gallery

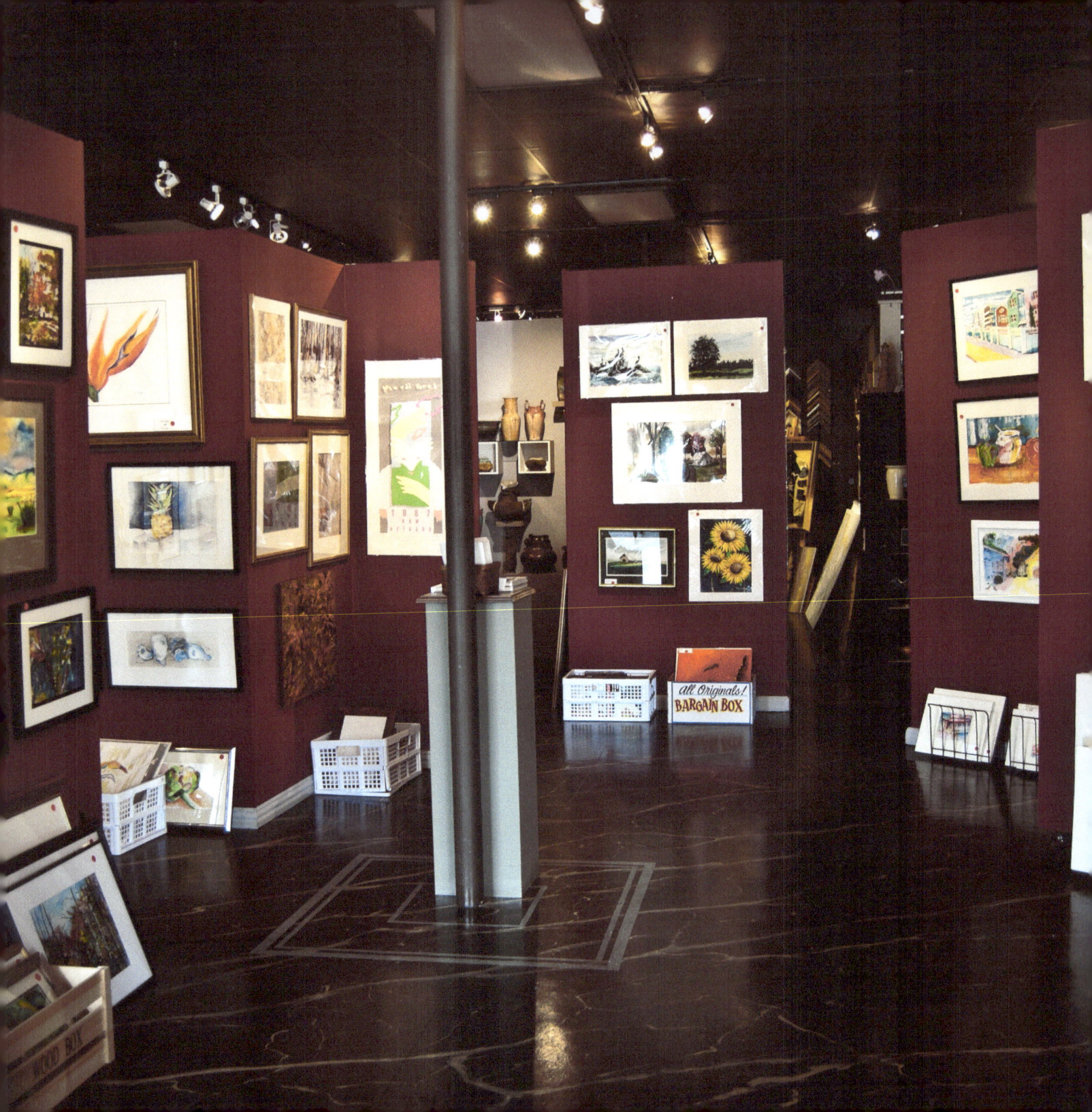

THE FRAMESHOP GALLERY 912

912 Coolidge Boulevard — Lafayette

Located in another spoke of the Hub City, The FrameShop Gallery 912 has been around since 1974. It sits on a main boulevard of the Oil Center.

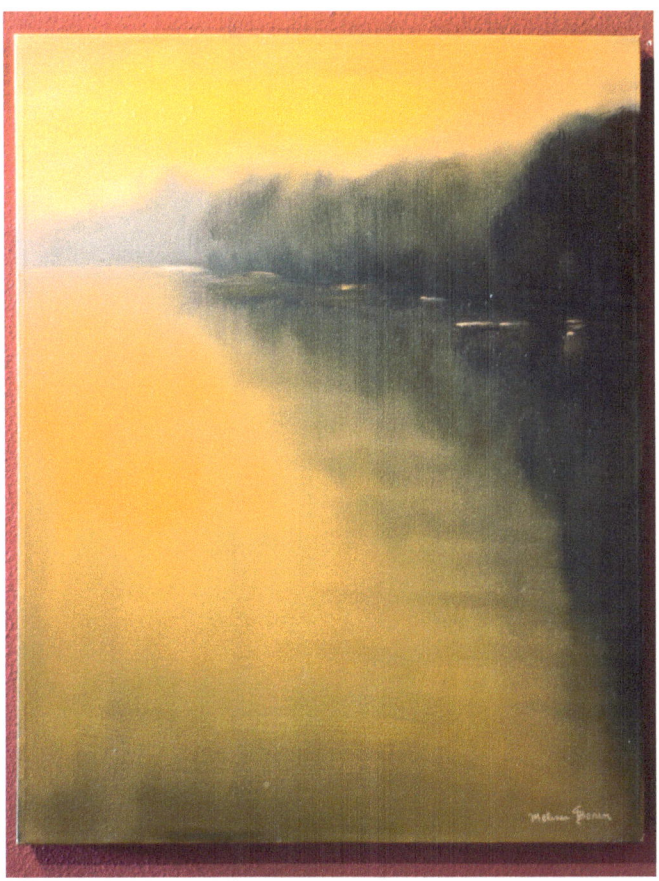

Above: You'll find a variety of fine art in a range of styles including those from local favorite Barbara Bonin, who painted this piece.

Left: The FrameShop is a great place to find and extensive range of abstract, fine art, photography and watercolor by local artists.

Like many galleries who have to support themselves with secondary offerings, framing helps owner Roger Laurent keep the doors open. But don't let the frames fool you. Within the walls of The FrameShop, artists push boundaries with their organized play of color and form.

You'll be wowed by the range of talent. Feel free to speak up as you browse the fine art gallery (I asked question after question about each artist). I could have spent hours absorbing the creative flare and detail in this gallery. Look for the deep and elegant work of Lynda Freese, Philip Gould, Louise Guidry, John Verly Richard and Tom Ladousa.

INSIDER'S TIP

Many small town galleries are traditionally closed on Sunday. FrameShop goers know this is the perfect day for afternoon conversations in the gallery, often directly with the artists, so be sure to ask Roger about the Sunday calendar.

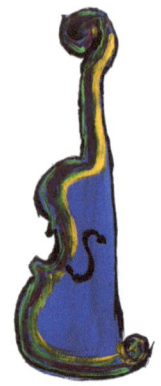

Teche Trial

The Bayou Teche flows lazily through several parishes east of Lafayette. Trail Teche follows the galleries in that region, flowing primarily through the self-proclaimed crawfish capital of the world, Breaux Bridge.

Breaux Bridge's downtown is a funky-cool, hand-painted wonder hidden just south of I-10 and a few minutes east of Lafayette. The area has more culture compressed in its small space than most people ever expect. You'll hear locals saying, "Big culture for a small town, cher!" And they're right.

The place is filled with an assortment of galleries, restaurants, antique shops, flea markets, ringing church bells and good old street talk. Just people-watching in Breaux Bridge will put a smile on your face. The town gets its name from a historic bridge commonly used as a directional landmark. When traveling and directions were given, folks would say, "Go to Breaux's bridge ..." This eventually became the city's name.

The trail runs south to historic St. Martinville, the oldest and first Cajun settlement. The town's spin on antebellum charm is intoxicating and it's home to the Evangeline Oak, made famous by Longfellow's poem Evangeline.

The Teche Trail makes for a big day so get an early start. Your first stop opens for breakfast and a famous brunch to keep you trailing all day. For that reason, the best day for Trail Teche is always Saturday.

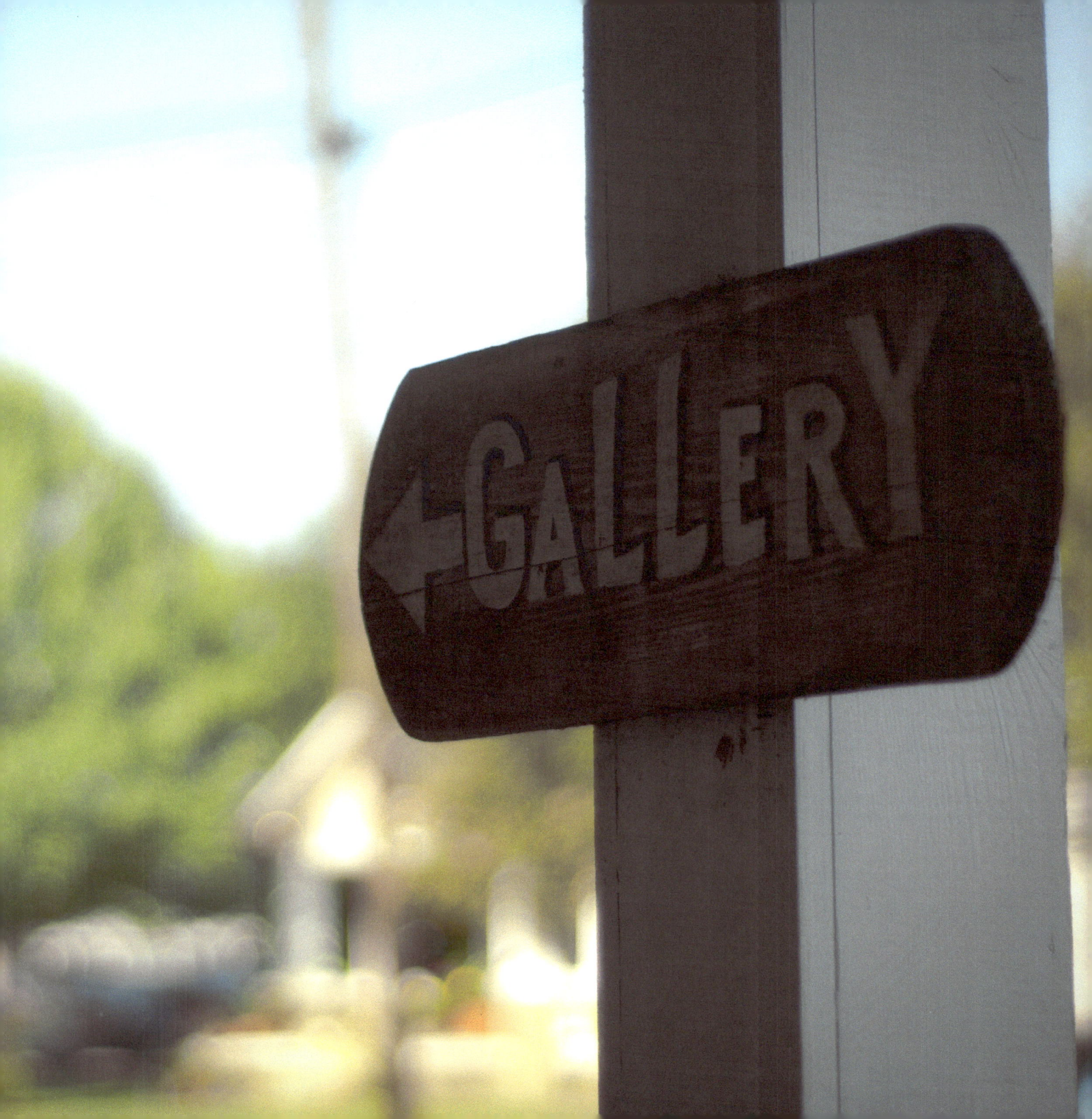

CAFÉ DES AMIS

140 East Bridge Street — Breaux Bridge

What do you get when you convert and old general merchandise store into a restaurant, bar and art gallery? Café Des Amis (Café of Friends).

Start your day here with breakfast and, if you're lucky, you'll catch the Saturday brunch with live local entertainment and a crowd of locals who kick off each Saturday with dancing and mimosas.

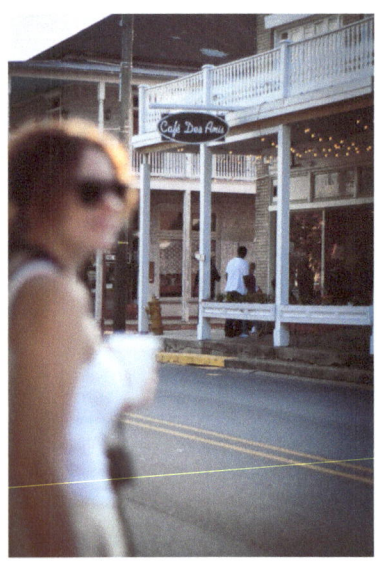

Above: Author Kelli Foret starts her day at Café Des Amis. The restaurant features a wealth of local visual art, great food and live zydeco and Cajun dancing every Saturday morning.

Right: Rue du Pont provides a peaceful place to relax and absorb a range of artistic styles.

The building dates back to 1890 and still has many artifacts from its original general merchandise days. Today its famous for food and music, but don't miss the great local art featured on the café walls. You'll feel the history of Breaux Bridge in its creaky floors and you stare at the work of local artists like Toby Rodriguez and Kelly Guidry. It's a combination of incredible cuisine, live music, Cajun dancing and local art that you won't find on any other trail.

RUE DU PONT

123 East Bridge Street — Breaux Bridge

Cross the street from Café des Amis into the quiet, intimate, room-to-room gallery of Rue Du Pont. The contrast takes you into another world with tranquil background sounds that seem to breathe life into the beautiful artwork.

Take in the fine art by local artists Kelli Kaufman, Lue Svendson, Candice Greer, Hope Hebert, Hannah Lane, Julie Breaux, and Tony Bernard. The front porch is a great place to absorb the breeze and relax with ice tea as you digest the peacefulness of the space and romantic expressions.

INSIDER'S TIP

Rue Du Pont is usually closed during the month of August so plan your visit during the cooler months of the year.

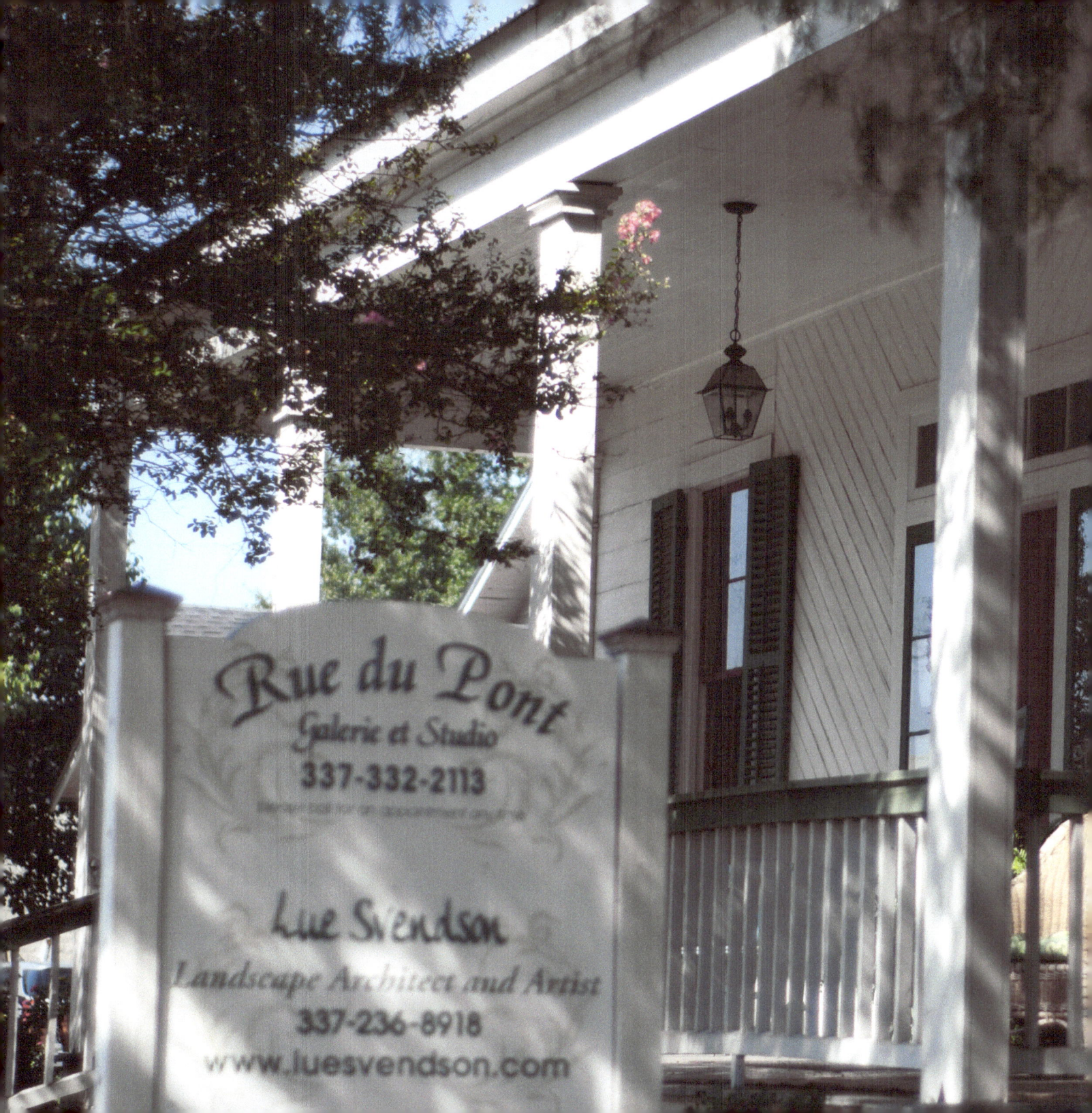

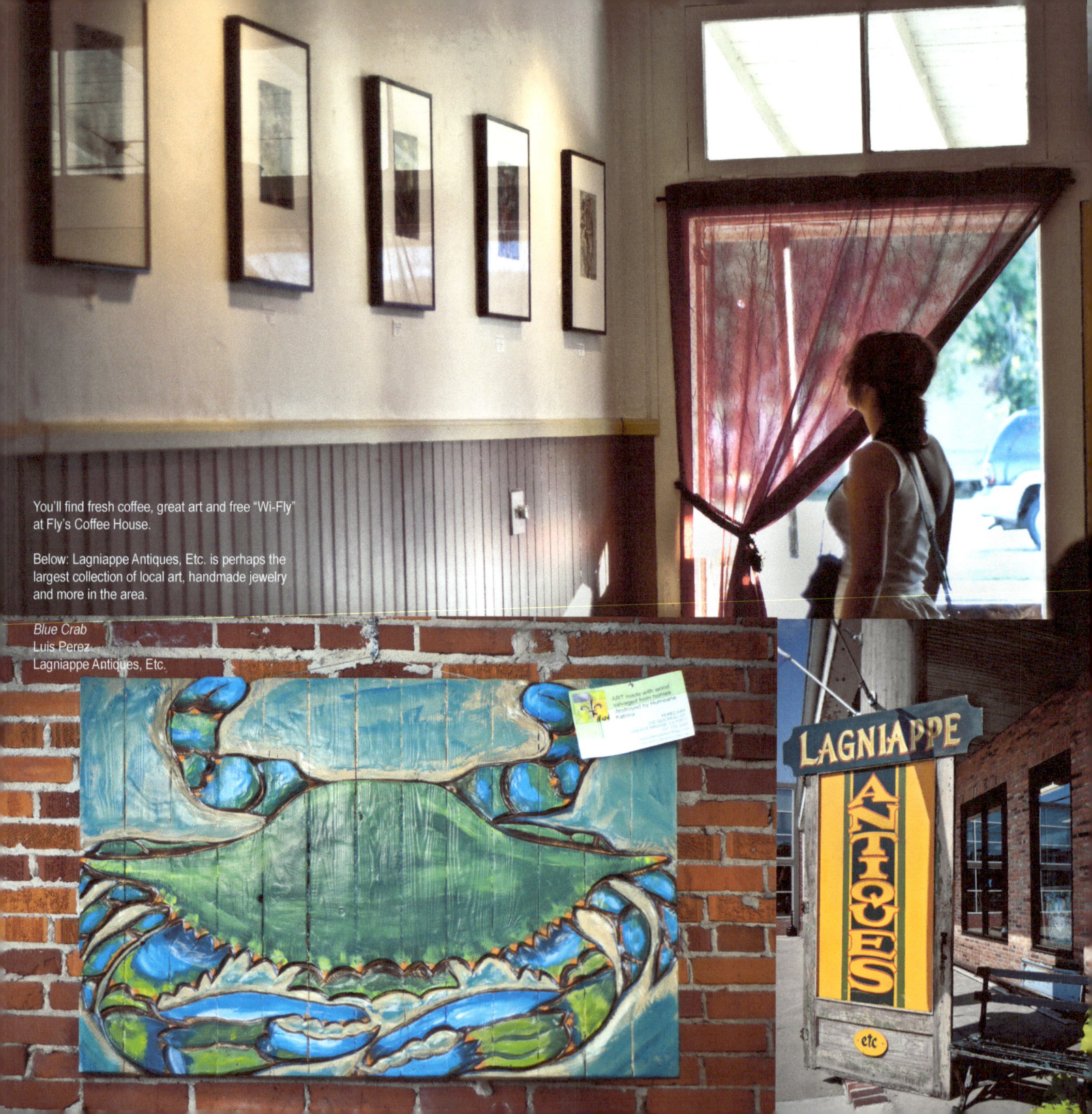

You'll find fresh coffee, great art and free "Wi-Fly" at Fly's Coffee House.

Below: Lagniappe Antiques, Etc. is perhaps the largest collection of local art, handmade jewelry and more in the area.

Blue Crab
Luis Perez
Lagniappe Antiques, Etc.

LAGNIAPPE ANTIQUES, ETC.

124 West Bridge Street — Breaux Bridge

Anyone who goes to Breaux Bridge can be distracted by the wonderful food. I call it eating my way across town. So after brunch and perhaps a dessert, it's time to walk off breakfast and Lagniappe Antiques is the perfect place.

Don't let the name fool you (I joke that the "Etc." stands for art). Sure, it's full of antiques. And by full, I mean 17,000 square feet of antiques. But the space doubles as a gallery for local artists Samuel Schwartz, Suzanne Chalotte, Leslie Leon Packer, Brian Miller, Barbara Connor, Troy Leleaux, Harriat Bloom, Janelle Hebert, Michalene Mouton, Wortman Pottery, Kelly Guidry and Luis Perez. You'll find an assortment of exquisite handmade jewelry, local photography scenes and sculpture infused with South Louisiana flair.

FLY'S COFFEE HOUSE

109 North Main Street — Breaux Bridge

So you've walked off brunch. Now it's time for a cup of coffee. Conveniently, Fly's is just across the street and it's our next gallery stop.

Take a moment to relax in this lively, Cajun spot and you'll change the way you think about coffee houses. Cajun/Zydeco music blares from a radio and it somehow seems more peaceful than any chain place filled with quietude and headphones. Listen to the conversations. Get to know the fiddler on the porch. Watch for the bird flying in to get a peek of what's happening.

If coffee's not your first choice, fill your belly with Ms. Glenda's lemon cake and raspberry ice tea. This place puts smiles on everyone's faces. You'll find the relaxed and informal art is often a reflection of the town's laissez-faire attitude. Even the locals seem lost in its atmosphere.

KELLY GUIDRY'S GALLERY/STUDIO

Van Buren Street — Breaux Bridge

What may seem like a just home is actually secondary to Art Gallery/Studio for local art celebrity, Kelly Guidry. This one's worth digging around for.

Make your way to Van Buren St. in Breaux Bridge and look for an eclectic style artist's home showcasing the bossy words, "Be Nice or Leave." At this point, you're just a knock on the door away from an art trailer's wonderland as the masculine and feminine worlds of Kelly Guidry collide to create masterpieces like no other.

Kelly is a chainsaw artist and his "living room" is also his gallery that overflows into an outdoor studio. Each screw, nail and knickknack has its own place in Guidry's assorted space. The laundry room even has a double purpose in this rough and rustic gallery. This is the out-of-the-way find only art trailers get to enjoy and it's worth every effort.

PEREZ ART AND FLAG

202 Guilbeau Street — Breaux Bridge

Just a block from Van Buren Street, Perez Art and Flag features "Three dimensional pieces of art from wood and tin that is handcrafted and colorful with unique details" — all works of Luis Perez.

Luis' wife Andrea, opened the business under the name The Trading Post. The retired teacher sought to combine a business and a hobby by following her passion for collecting antiques and collectables. When she met Louis and they married, she began selling his personal works of flavor.

Luis hand carves wood taken from the streets of New Orleans post Katrina. Some of his most famous pieces are what he calls his "Katrina crosses". Luis and his work are a little "out of the box", which makes this gallery a perfect stop for Art Trailers!

INSIDER'S TIP

Ask Andrea to see Luis' "Dr. John Voodoo piece"… you'll love it!

Top Right: Kelly Guidry's home doubles as a gallery and studio.

Bottom Right: Perez Art and Flag carries a range of items and features the mixed-media artwork of Luis Perez.

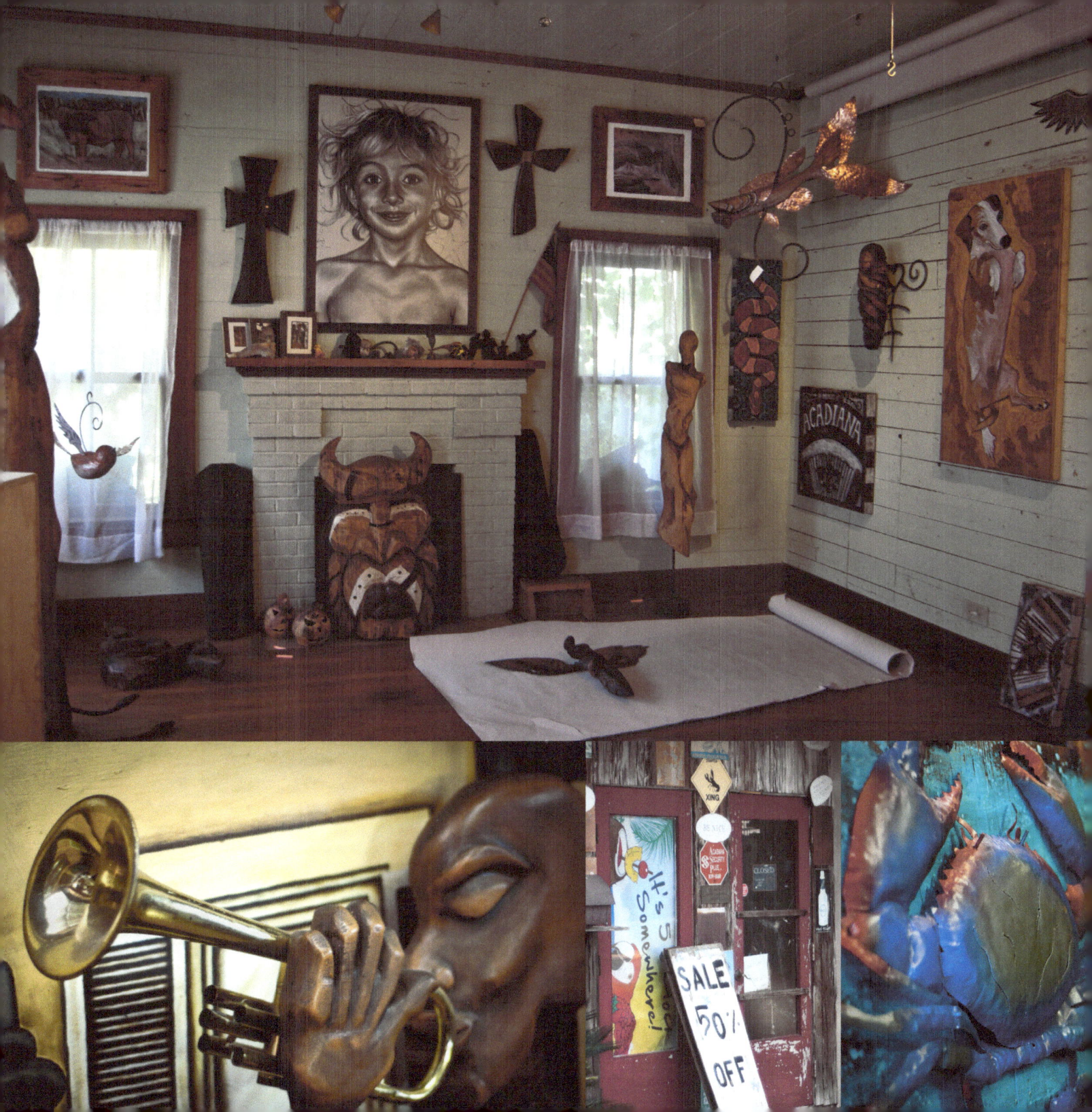

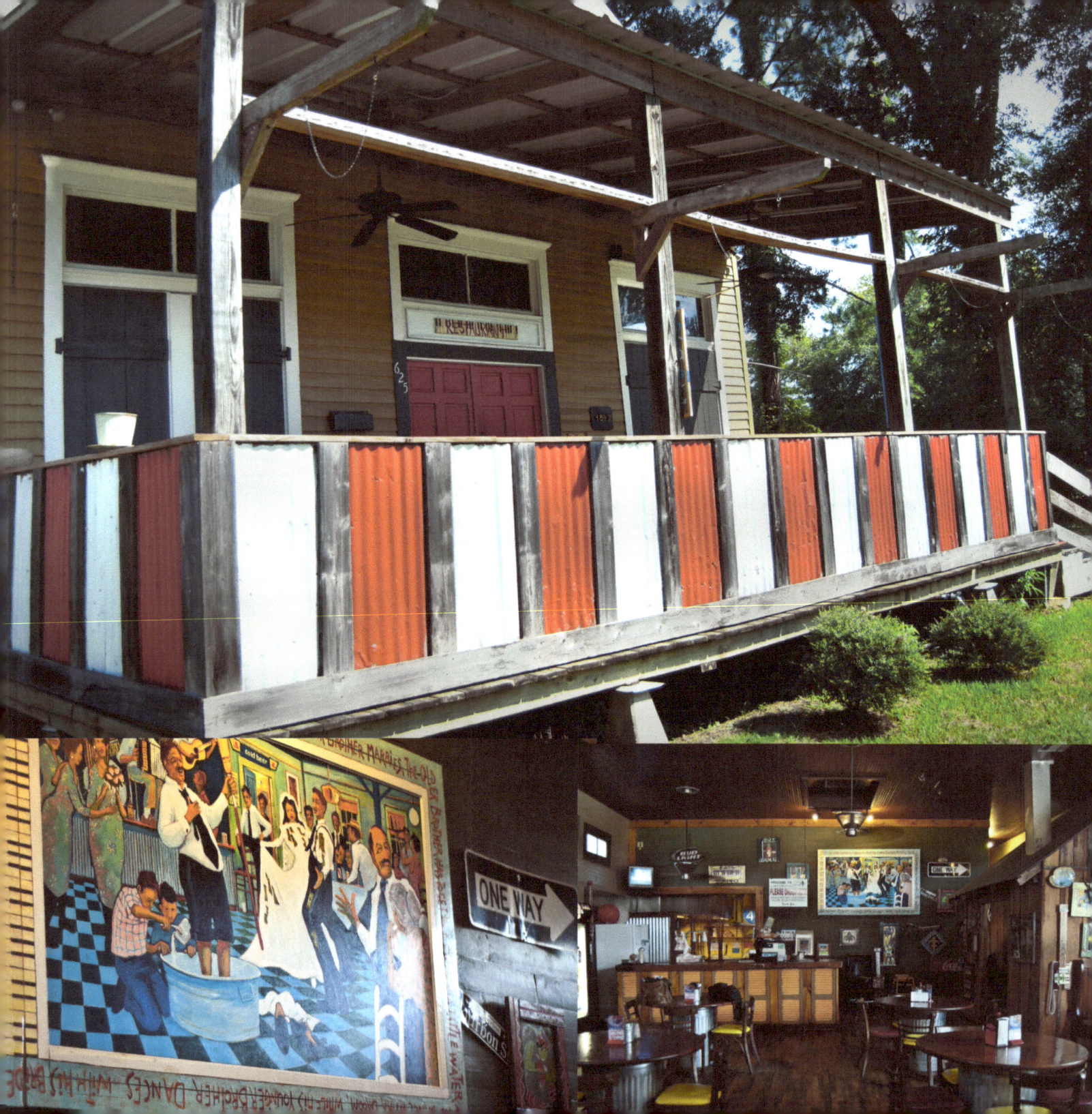

CORNER BAR POOR-BOYS

625 Grand Point Avenue — Breaux Bridge

Is it time for lunch yet? Our next stop is another great "art-eatery" on Trail Teche called Corner Bar Poor Boys. Small town exhibition halls almost always share a dual purpose and this one's second calling is serving up delicious home style Cajun food. What art trailers will love is how the walls are littered with Boogie Hebert's canvas expressions of local life.

The beaded wood walls contrast the artist's acrylic on canvas showcase of local African-American culture familiar to Hebert's childhood. Most scenes depict real-life experiences. His father and local artist Earl Hebert influenced Boogie to paint larger than life memories of old traditions like gathering in the streets and fishing on the bayou. From the burlap curtains flowing in the breeze to the Mardi Gras Beads dangling from the window above, this tiny café is a refreshing (and filling) stop for local folk art.

DUCHAMP OPERA HOUSE

200 South Main Street — St. Martinville

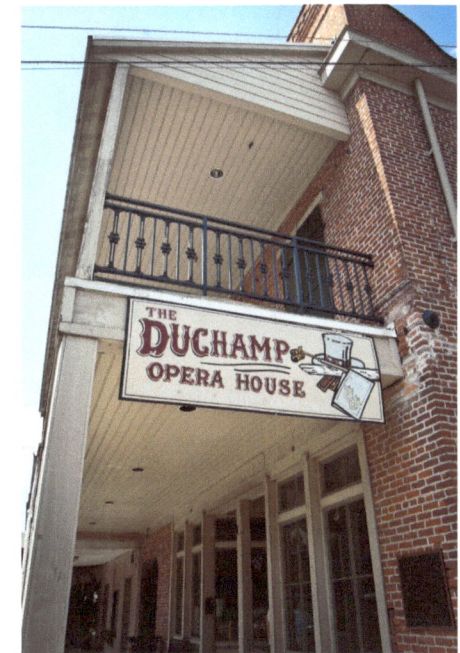

The Duchamp Opera House and Mercantile of St. Martinville was once a fully operational, 19th century opera center. Restored to its original form, this beautiful building houses eclectic art from Adrian Fulton, Nolan Barras, Lou Jarrell and more. It's very common to find an artist or two painting in the gallery itself, an incredible opportunity for art trailers who want to understand the inspiration behind their works.

Left: Corner Bar Poor-Boys is a lively, decorative and authentic Cajun eatery filled with local (and sometimes humorous) artwork.

Right: Duchamp Opera House's first floor hosts a range of local art in a variety of expressions. The second floor is home to locally produced plays. Call ahead for show times.

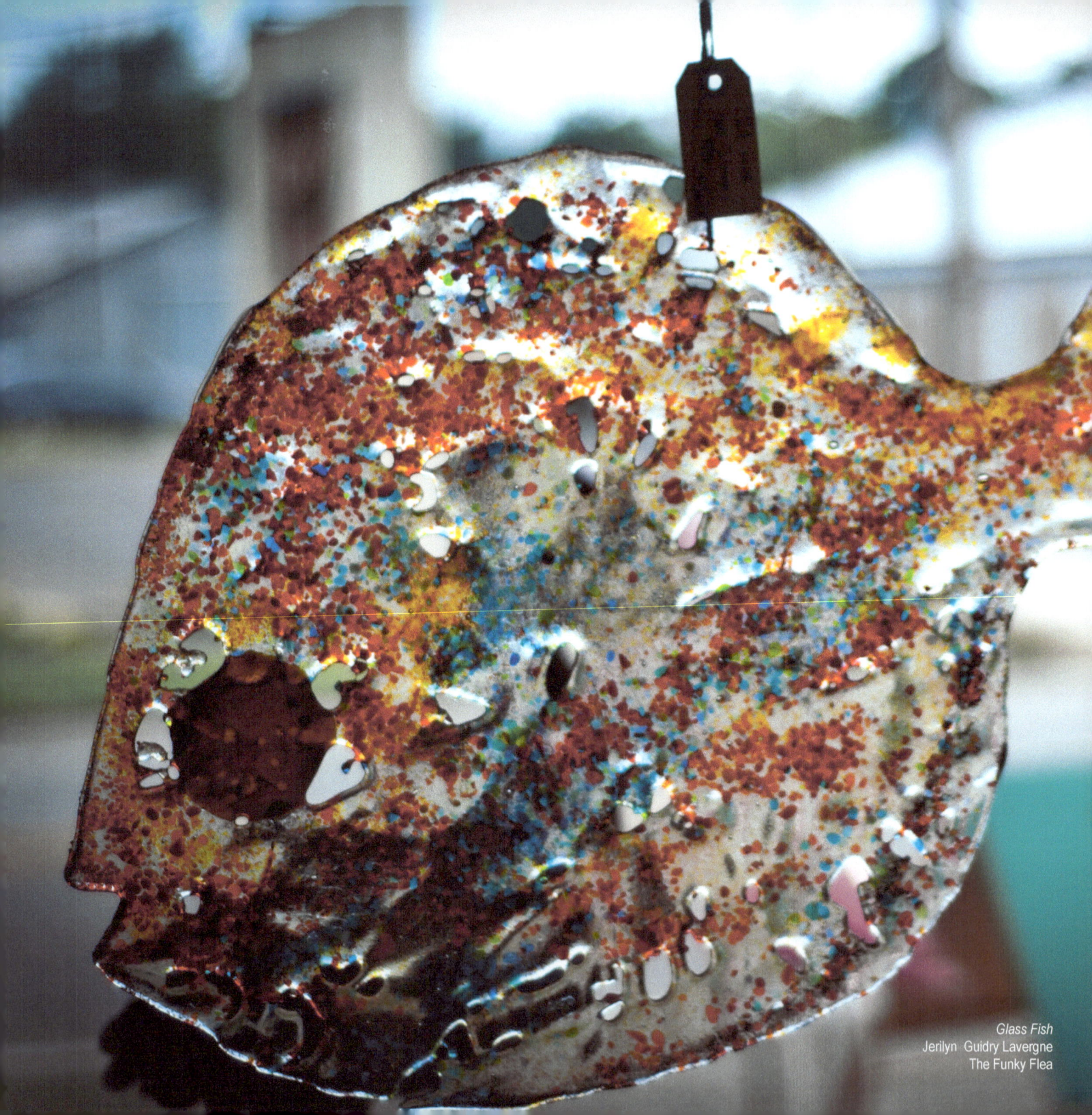

Glass Fish
Jerilyn Guidry Lavergne
The Funky Flea

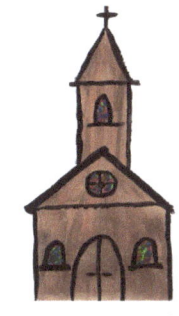

Prairie Trail

If you're looking for a slower paced trail, the Prairie Trail is definitely it. It's got the simple way of life written all over it.

Your first stop is in Eunice, where you could possibly spend more than a day or two. This town probably houses more museums and cultural centers per capita than any other. You'll find city museums, federally supported national historical parks, cultural centers, performing arts venues and The Cajun Music Hall of Fame all within a short radius. The prairie is rich in history and culture. Seasonally, Eunice is well known for its Cajun Music and Courir de Mardi Gras (an ancient rural Mardi Gras custom), but it definitely has its share of visual arts to take in.

The trail continues to Sunset, home of the locally popular Garden and Herb Festival each May. Once known as the sweet potato capital of the world, this little village has earned its spot among Acadiana's most culturally enriched towns. Flea markets and antique shops stand along the main drag and you'll find no shortage of treasure hunters browsing vintage paraphernalia.

As Art Trailers, we focused on the not-so-mainstream, not-so-easy-to-find locations with interesting, eclectic art. Trust me, Eunice and Sunset are a find. Take your time and take in the sites just about any Wednesday through Saturday. Those are great days for the Prairie Trail. However, it's worth making a special appointment for Le Village as this venue only opens one Monday a month to the public.

Café Mosaic

202 South 2nd Street — Eunice

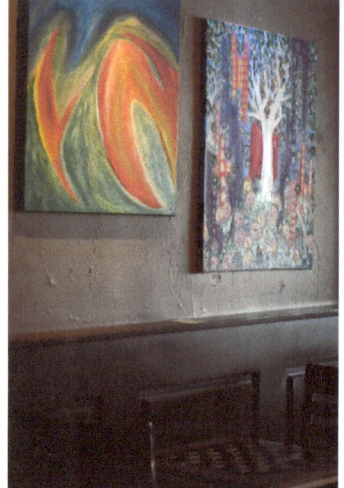

Above: You'll find a range of local art at Café Mosaic. Many of the pieces are by students at the nearby college, such as these two paintings by Beth Guidry who studies at LSUE.

Right Top: Le Village's gallery is tucked into the wooded outskirts of Eunice and well worth the drive.

Right Bottom: Café Mosaic is a favorite place for young and old. Don't forget to indulge in their latte art.

Once again, small galleries in small towns often serve multiple functions. While Café Mosaic may look like a coffee house on the outside, this little nook serves as an informal arts and cultural center for the town of Eunice.

As Eunice's only coffee house, the café brings in old and young alike, mixing and conversing on topics that range from photography to farming. You'll delight in the fine art and photos that decorate the walls of this big-city-style coffee house.

Not only does this coffee house give locals a place to flaunt their art, but it also engages in a little coffee art of their own ... latte art. Owner, Nathanael Johnson, is classified by the Specialty Coffee Association of America as the highest ranking barista in the state. Latte art is a skill he perfected during the process. Ask him to showcase his talents when you're there.

INSIDER'S TIP

Contact Nathanael in advance of your visit to find out if you can catch one of their regular open mic nights, poetry readings and book signings.

INSIDER'S TIP

Plan ahead for the second Monday of the month. That's "Market Monday" where you can get lunch, cold drinks and unique finds.

Le Village

121 Seale Lane — Eunice

Doubling as a bed and breakfast, Le Village General Store provides a venue for local artisans to display and sell artwork and crafts. When you drive down the gravel road to Le Village you'll feel a mystic excitement build. The reward: A back-in-time market atmosphere as you arrive. You'll love the local handmade crafts, photography, and fine art that are all part of a bygone scene here at Le Village.

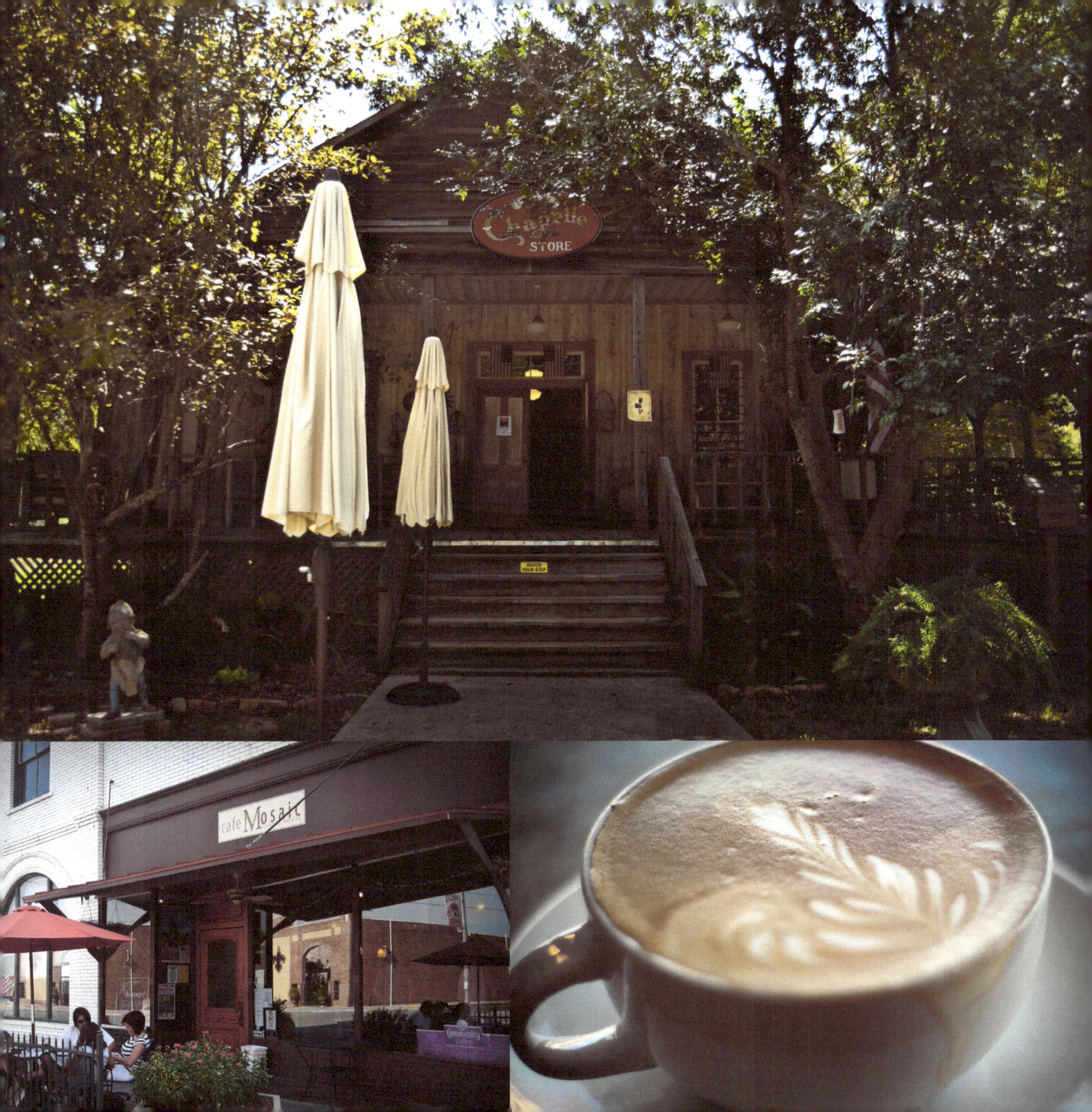

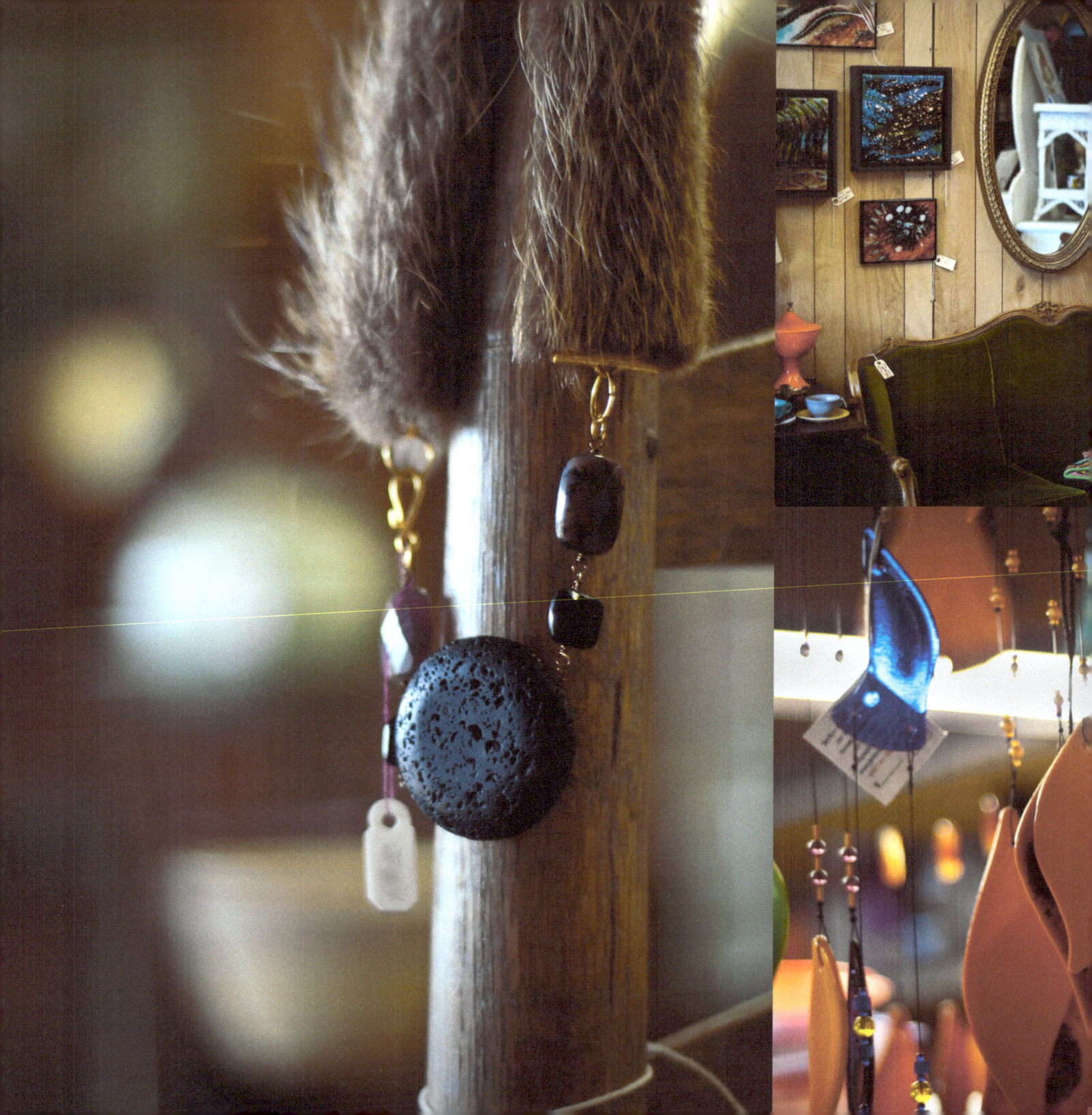

THE FUNKY FLEA

829-A Napoleon Avenue — Sunset

How do you beat a place with a name like The Funky Flea? It's just intriguing enough to make an Art Trailer go crazy. And let me tell you, this place has some unique finds. How about a nutria necklace, for starters? You'll appreciate the fine paintings … on saw blades. There's plenty of other quirky folk art, too.

The name of this venue truly tells all. It's not just a flea market. It's not just a funky art gallery. It's both and everything in-between. The venue alone is out-of-the-ordinary enough to visit.

Shop owners Claudette Simon, Talli LeBouef and Dr. Whitney Broussard opened for business just a few short months ago and wasted no time proving their Art Trail cred with collections of funky, fascinating works. This one's a tickle.

JERILYN'S GLASS STUDIO

287 Pershing Highway — Sunset

Trek a little further into Sunset for a sampling of local glass art. "If I'm home, I'm open!" exclaims Jerilyn. She'll greet you with a hug and a kiss and proudly walk you through her fused glass expressions. Ask about how her glass turns into fun and how her dream became a reality in her own backyard. Jerilyn's style is unplanned. As she says, she doesn't make things, they just happen.

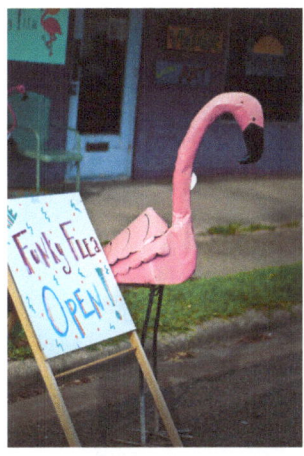

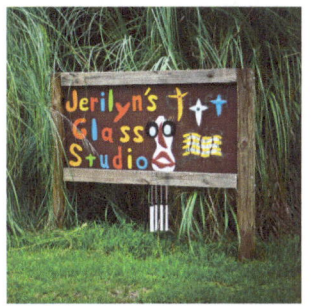

Above: To help you find each of these locations, The Funky Flea and Jerilyn's have put their on spin on decorative signs.

Far Left: One of the more unique artistic expressions at The Funky Flea — nutria fur jewelry.

Left Top: The Funky Flea, as you might have guessed, was originally a funky flea-market. According to the owners, local art has been incredibly popular.

Left Bottom: Jerilyn's glass chimes have been known to survive hurricanes and are a great way to introduce color and sound to almost any space.

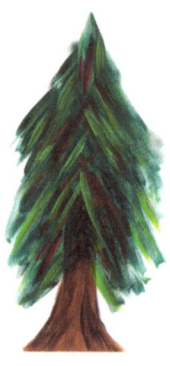

Coteau Trail

An attraction for anyone seeking anything historic and magnificent, Grand Coteau, Louisiana reigns in visitors from all over the world. Eager to get a taste of the town's architecture, landscape, great food and religious background, Grand Coteau is on the top of the list for any traveler touring Acadiana. While this town attracts tourists and locals alike combing the historic sites, don't let it fool you. Grand Coteau has plenty to offer in the arts. From The Festival of Words to filmmaking and visual arts, this town has ample culture to enjoy. Getting lost in the local shops, galleries and venues here is easy and a perfect retreat for an Art Trailer!

Just east of Grand Coteau lies "A haven for artists and musicians from around the world," Arnaudville, LA sits at the junction of the Bayou Tech and Bayou Fuselier in St. Landry and St. Martin parishes. Home to the Étouffée' Festival, Le Feu et l'Eau (Fire and Water Rural Arts Celebration) and Bayou Blues Revival, this quaint town got its start as the original site of an Attakapas Indian Village, and is one of the oldest remaining towns in St. Landry Parish. Maybe it's the spirits of the remaining Attakapas relics or maybe it's the flow of the teche churning up the lustrous soil, but whatever "it" is, Arnaudville definitely has it! Giving birth to shops like Tom's Fiddle and Bow, where regular Cajun jamming occurs or NuNu's, the town's rural arts center, Arnaudville is certainly a cultural magnet for creation along the Teche. Make your way to Arnaudville to discover its hidden relics and newest crop!

Coteau Trail is definitely a favorite! Wednesday through Saturday are great days to take the Coteau Trail. This trail is perfect for a relaxing afternoon and does not require a full day of trailing. Take advantage of the local shops Grand Coteau has to offer!

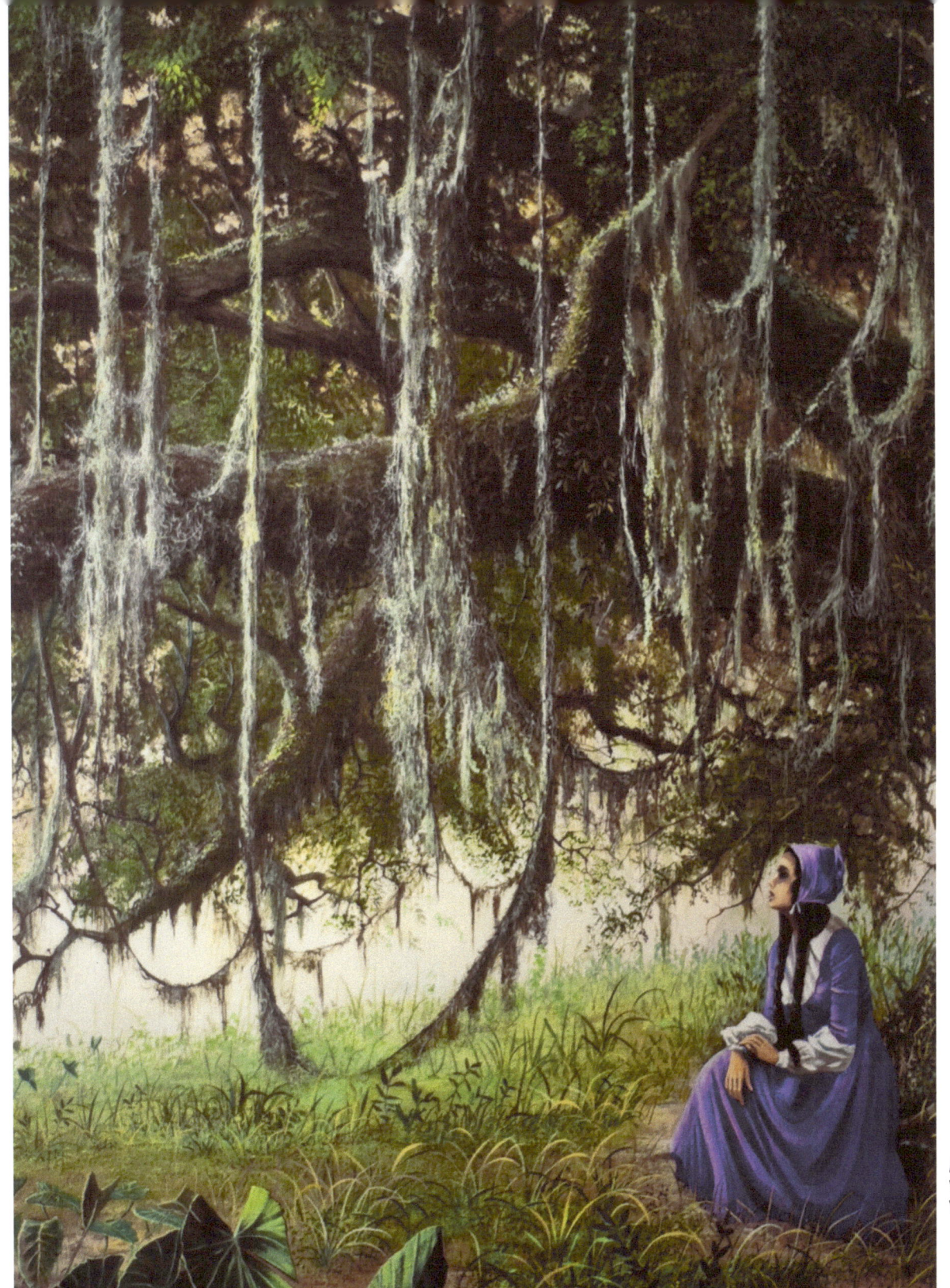

Evangeline
Vincent Darby
Vincent Darby Studio

45

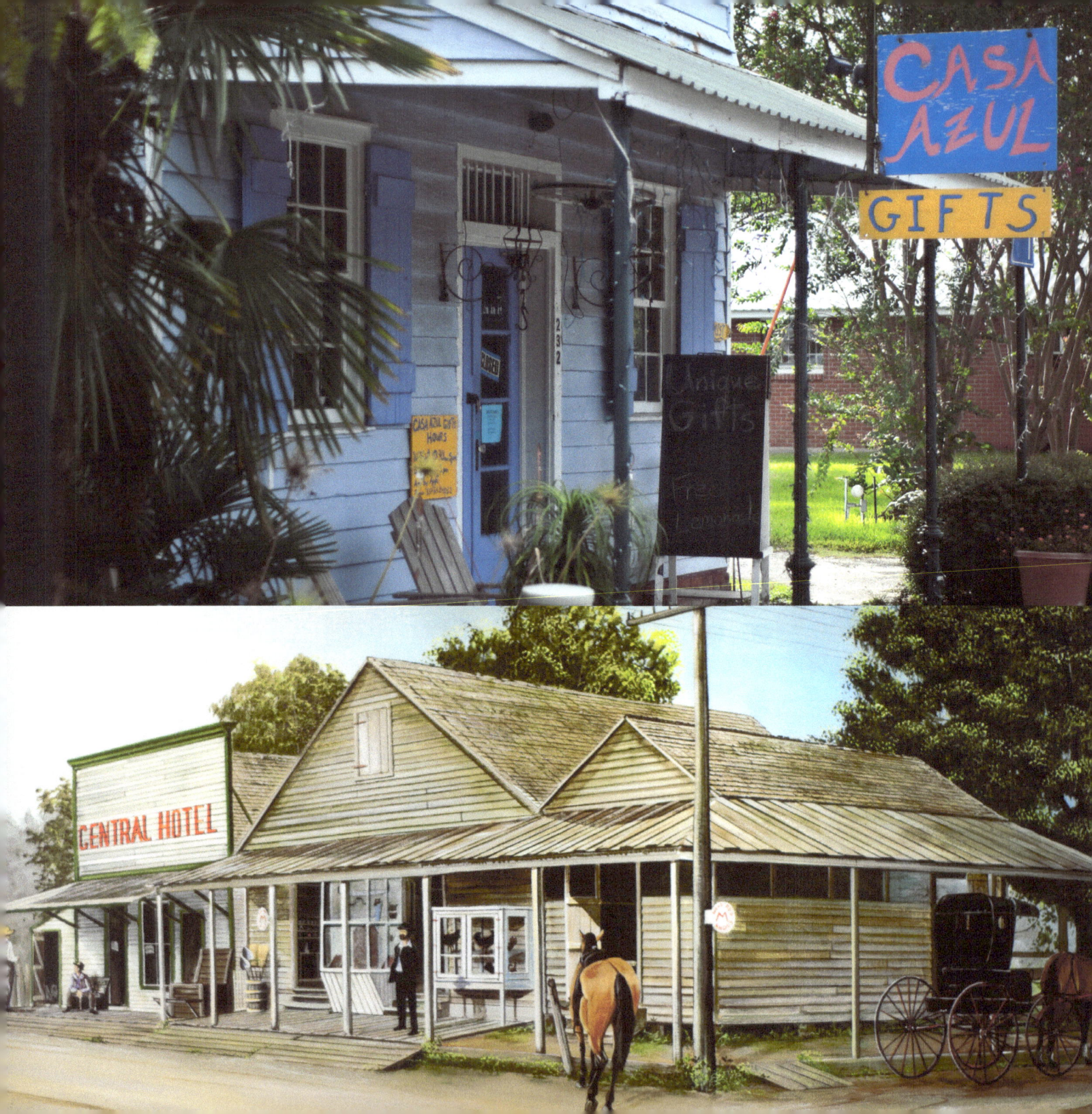

CASA AZUL

232 Martin Luther King Drive — Grand Coteau

Home to local art activist, Patrice Melnick, Casa Azul attracts every art form into its periwinkle blue doors. A place that exudes peace and harmony, Casa Azul brings to its back room writers, poets, filmmakers, musicians, craftsmen, and artists. The type of visual art here spans from Indian Block Printing to jewelry makers and fine art. While also a gift shop, Casa Azul hosts classes like Journaling Techniques, Quilt Making and Printing with Indian Wood Blocks. This cultural arts shop features local artists whose names you may recognize including Frank Thompson and Neketta Guillory. While local is what you can find, this shop owner brings a "global shopping experience" to Grand Coteau. Casa Azul is definitely an artist lover's space and a hit that tops the charts for Grand Coteau.

VINCENT DARBY'S ART STUDIO

400 Canal Street — Arnaudville

Detailed front porch scenes from days of old embedded in paintings of nature and wildlife is what you'll discover as you make your way into Vincent Darby's Art Studio. Darby's paintings tell a story of long ago when times seemed simpler. Twisting oak trees, hanging moss and untouched wildlife live in Darby's pieces. "I get lost in scenes of solitude and paradise," says Darby, "That's what inspires me." All scenes depict settings of what you'd find in south Louisiana.

I enjoyed my afternoon with Darby as he spoke of his work over fried chicken and ice cream. I learned that his career as a game warden in the Acadiana area led him to an old friend who loaned him his first set of paints. Between these and furniture paint from his father's furniture store, Darby was unstoppable. "I just didn't stop painting," says Darby. A visit at Vincent Darby's Art Studio is something that art trailers must do. There is a rocking chair waiting for you!

Top Left: Casa Azul offers locally made jewelry, visual art and gifts you'll find nowhere else. Ask about their schedule of readings, book signings and documentary nights.

Bottom Left: As you can see from this close-up, Vincent Darby's work can be incredibly detailed. Most people would never guess he was self-taught.

NuNu's
Arts & Culture Collective

1510 Bayou Courtableau Highway (Hwy. 93 East) — Arnaudville

INSIDER'S TIP

NuNu's always has something brewing so checkout their website or contact them ahead of time for functions that are alive with stripes!

What originated as a lumberyard and then a feed store, NuNu's new building is a perfect place for the vibe and feel of the one of a kind community center. After a fire last year burned the hard work of those involved in the Arnaudville Experiment that includes NuNu's, the community is almost complete in reviving their new space.

NuNu's is quite a collective including Frederick l'Ecole des Arts, Music of Acadiana Stage, Jacques Arnaud French Studies Collective, Deux Bayous Gallery, Atelier-Courtableau Artists' Collective, and Cafe' NuNu. The community of artists here are bubbling and exhibit mind-bending works that are sure to awaken your imagination.

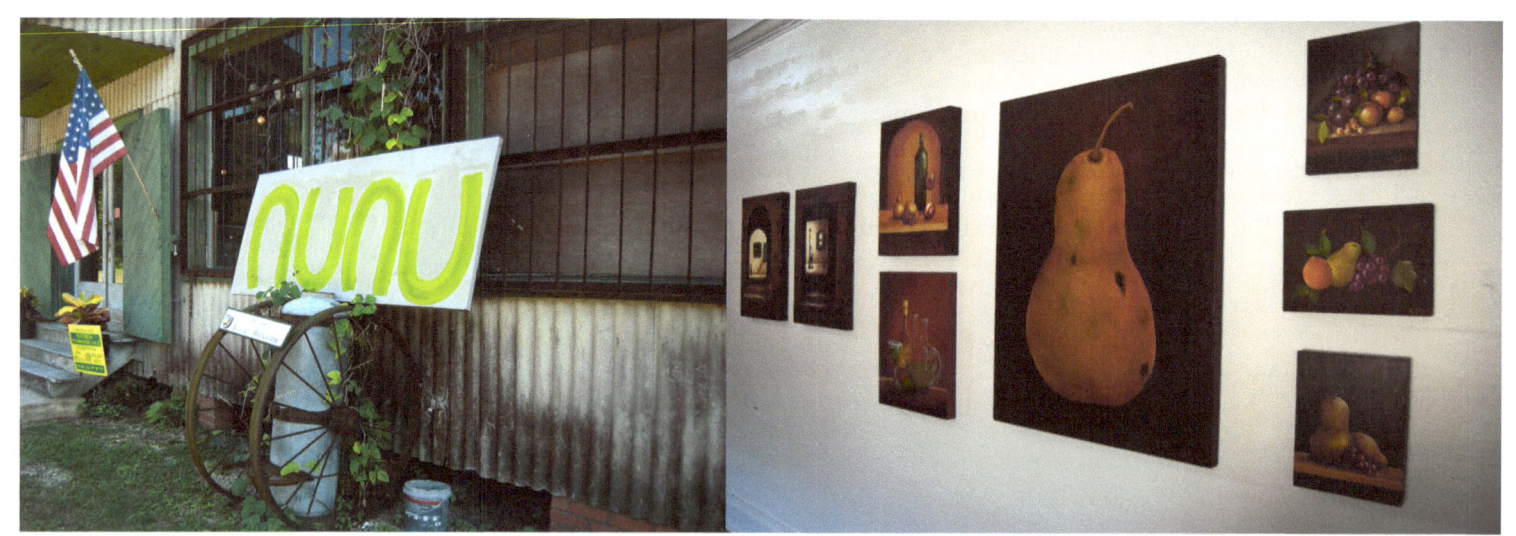

This collective is home to live events, artist discussions, art lessons and more.

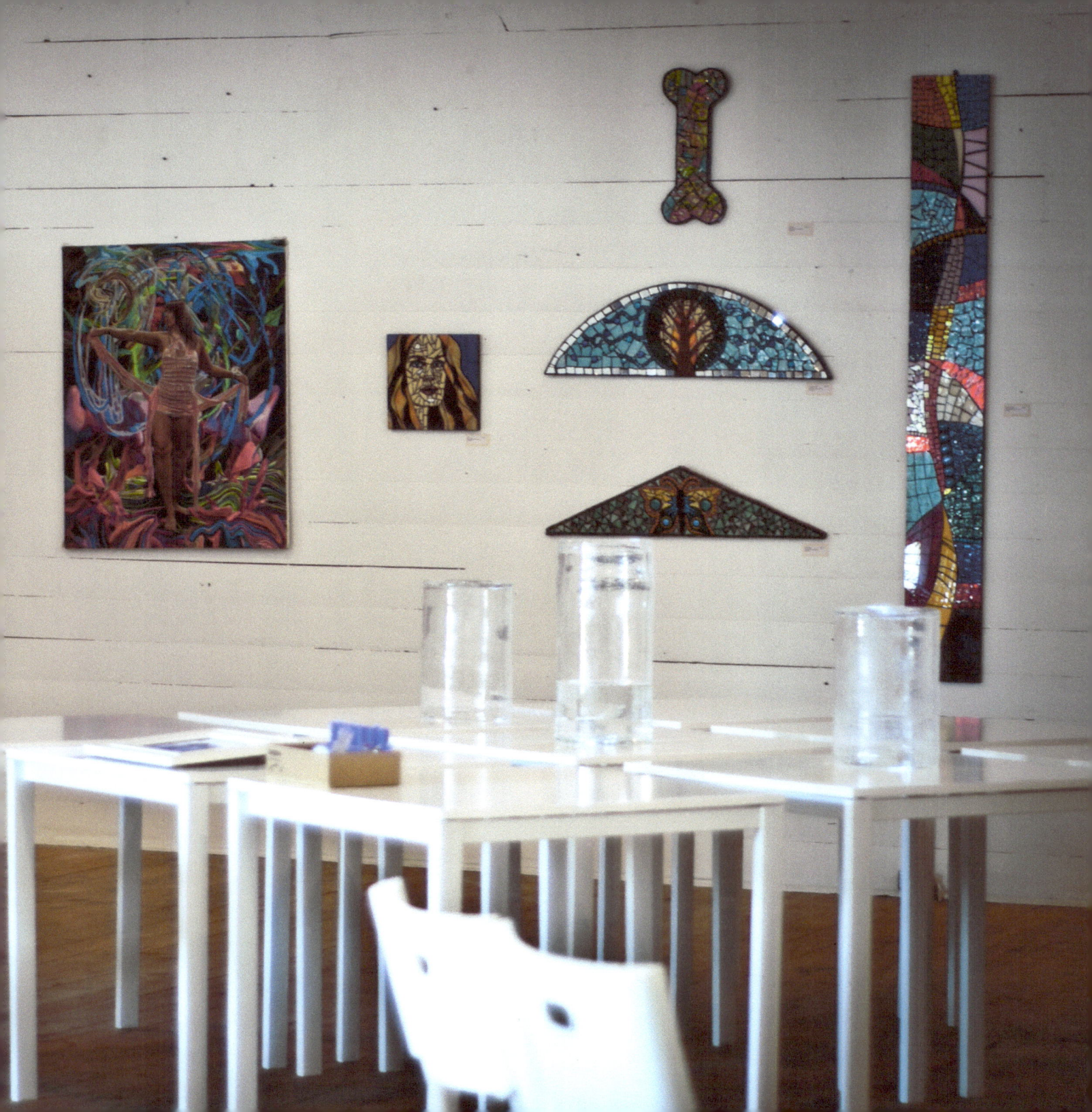

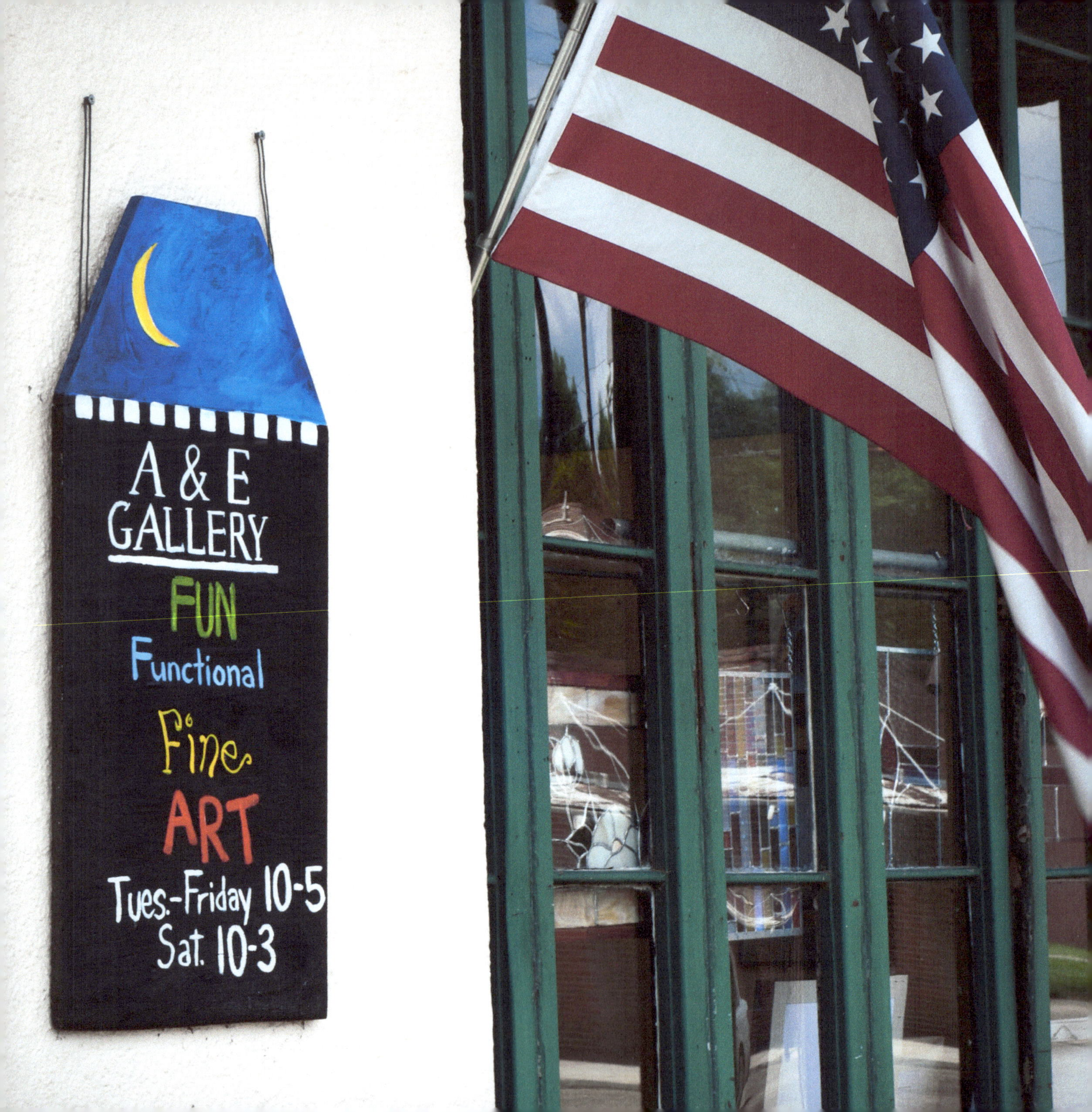

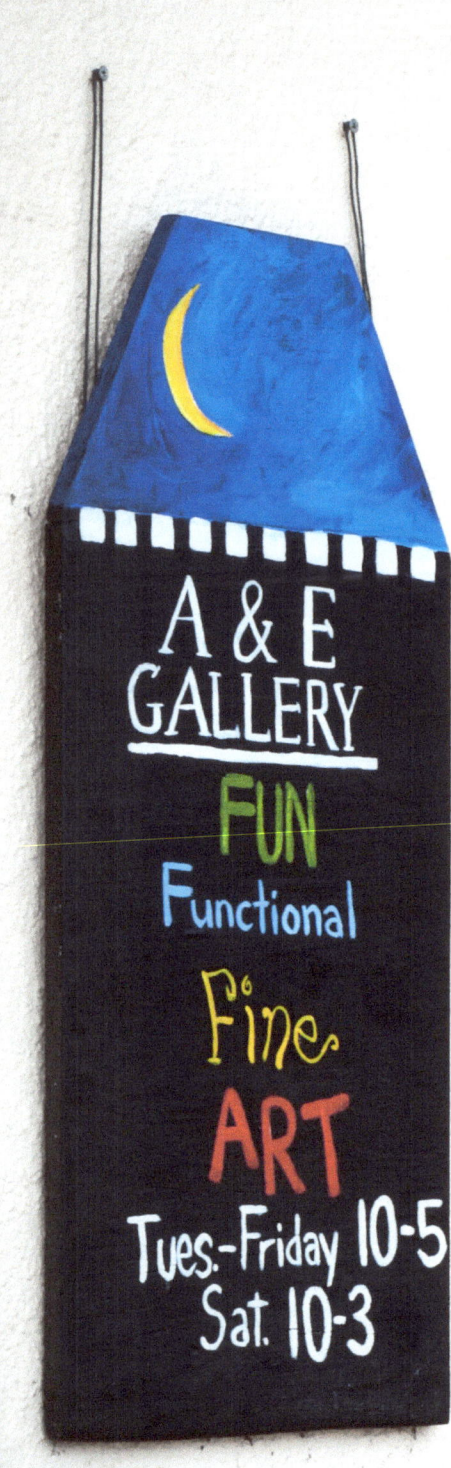

A & E
GALLERY

FUN

Functional

Fine

ART

Tues.-Friday 10-5
Sat. 10-3

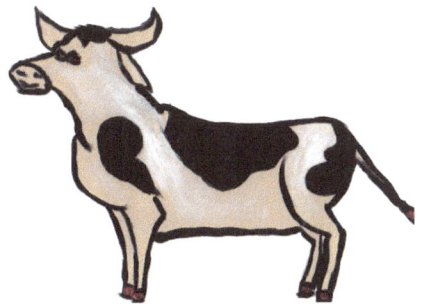

Vermilion Trail

Further down the Bayou Teche you'll find a rich history of Spanish culture steeped in sugar cane and seafood. Your first stop, the town of New Iberia, finds a place in Cajun story books and famous novels. It's home to the famous George Rodrigue, author James Lee Burke, Tabasco Hot Sauce, and the Sugar Cane Festival. This town has a wide-ranging mix of influences from Spanish to Creole, German to Cajun.

From there the trail turns west to Vermilion Parish. It's there you'll love the majesty of Abbeville's historic Magdalen Square and its surrounding galleries. Next, the drive from Abbeville to Gueydan will inspire you to roll your windows down, turn the radio up, and enjoy the country back roads that stretch as far as you can see. You'll arrive in Gueydan (pronounced: gay•don) for a cultural (and just plain unique) experience you won't find anywhere else. You'll turn north to Lafayette through the small town of Maurice for the final gallery on this trail — a trip through cow pastures and across cattle guards for a treasure fit for a Russian Czar.

Vermilion Trail is another low key, relaxing ride. Wednesday through Saturday is a great day to Vermilion Trail. Think of this trail as a classic road trip filled with long stretches of open road, as the locations can be spread out. Relax in your seat, bring your favorite music and enjoy the journey!

A&E GALLERY

335 West St. Peter's Street — New Iberia

Fun. Functional. Fine Art. That's Paul Schexnayder's A&E Gallery in a nutshell. View work from more than twenty local artists in the form of painting, sculpture, jewelry, woodworking and more. The incredibly large space — the warehouse used to be an auto dealership in the early 1900's — also houses "Painted Bayou," a series of painting workshops and classes. You can easily catch a series of brunches, theater performances, poetry readings, parties, socials and student art shows. This first stop on Vermilion Trail is full of options and one of the most spectacular galleries in the area.

INSIDER'S TIP

Look for my favorite Art Trailer quote, "It doesn't matter how the paint is put on, as long as something is said…" It's hidden.

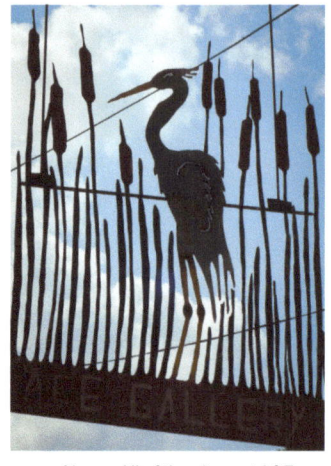

Above: All of the signs at A&E are handmade works of art.

Right: Be sure to check out Paul Schexnayder's *Barefoot Series*, his most recent production.

CLEMENTINE

113 East Main Street — New Iberia

The world-renowned Clementine Hunter's folk art inspires the name of one of New Iberia's hot spots for dining, cocktails and fun. Restaurateur Wayne Peltier named the place after his favorite artist and he displays many of her tribute works alongside other local favorites. You can dine and tour the latest exhibits New Iberia has to offer. Immerse yourself in the rich Creole cuisine, Louisiana scenes and Peltier's favorite — work that pays tribute to Clementine's simple kind of sign language she portrays.

INSIDER'S TIP

Call ahead for restaurant hours, as you'll want to catch Clementine for one of their amazing meals.

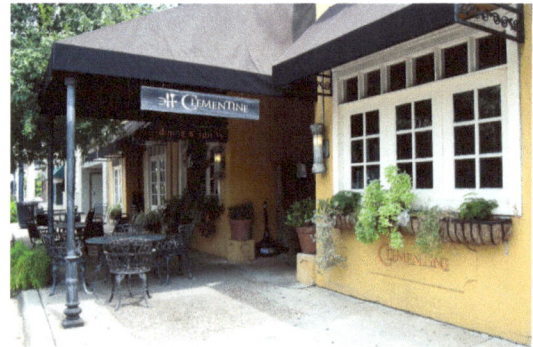

Above: Dining at Clementine is a treat, so plan to visit this restaurant/gallery during serving hours.

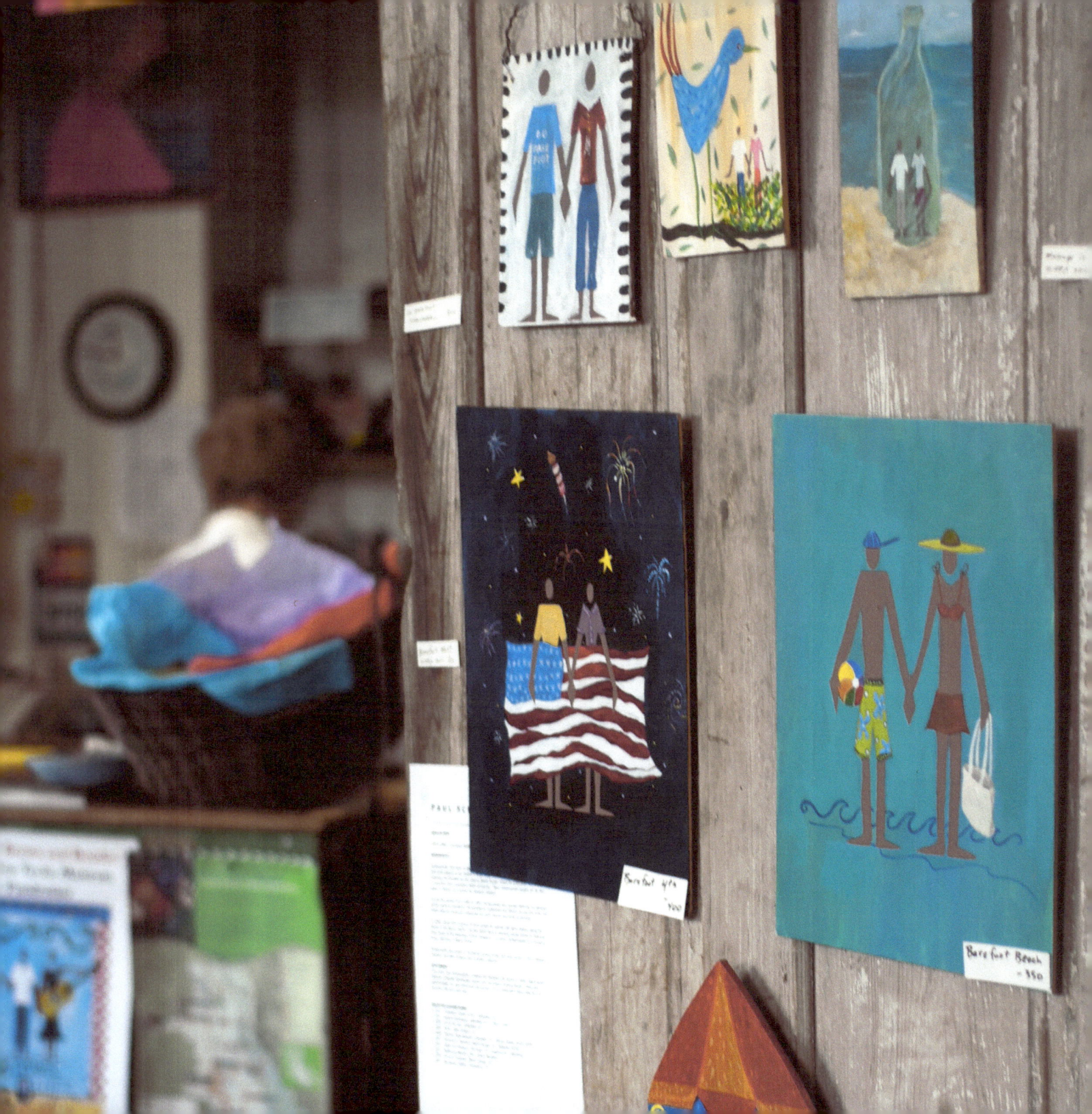

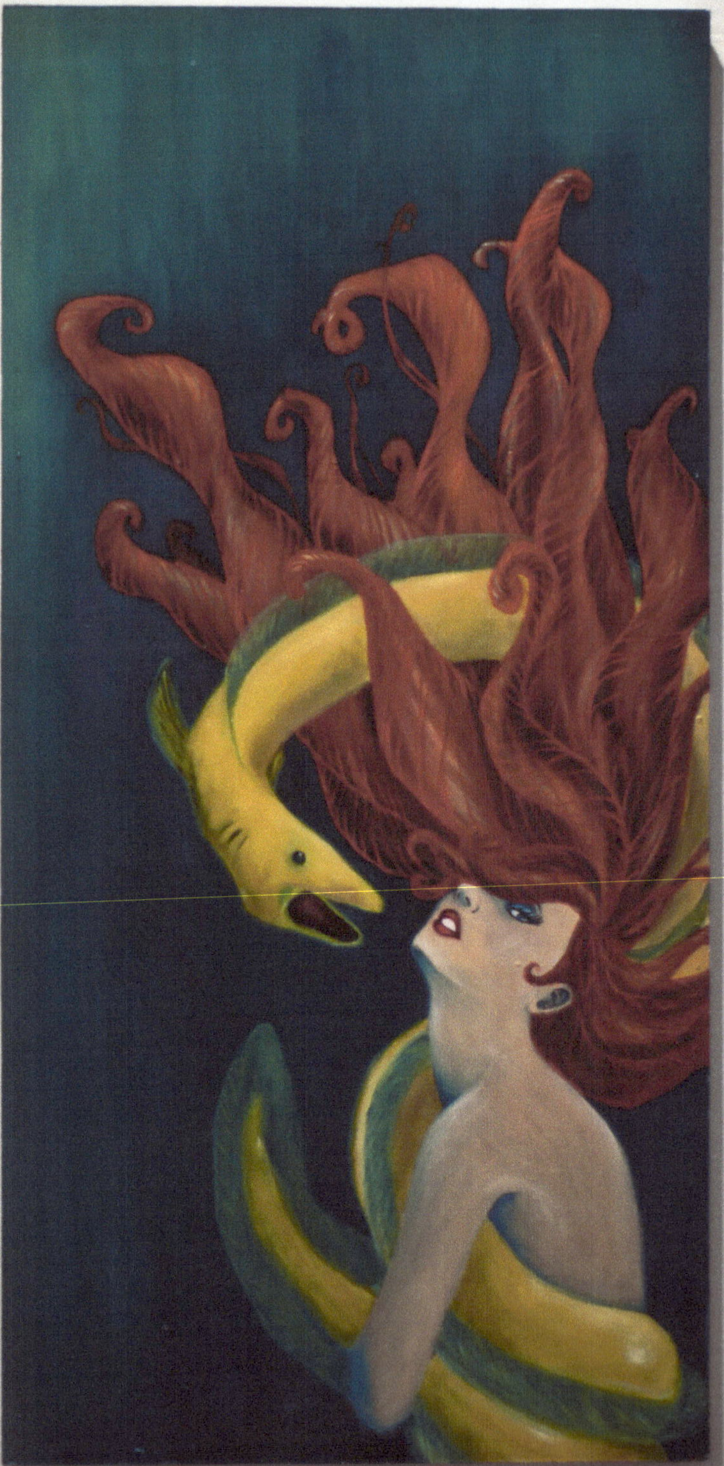

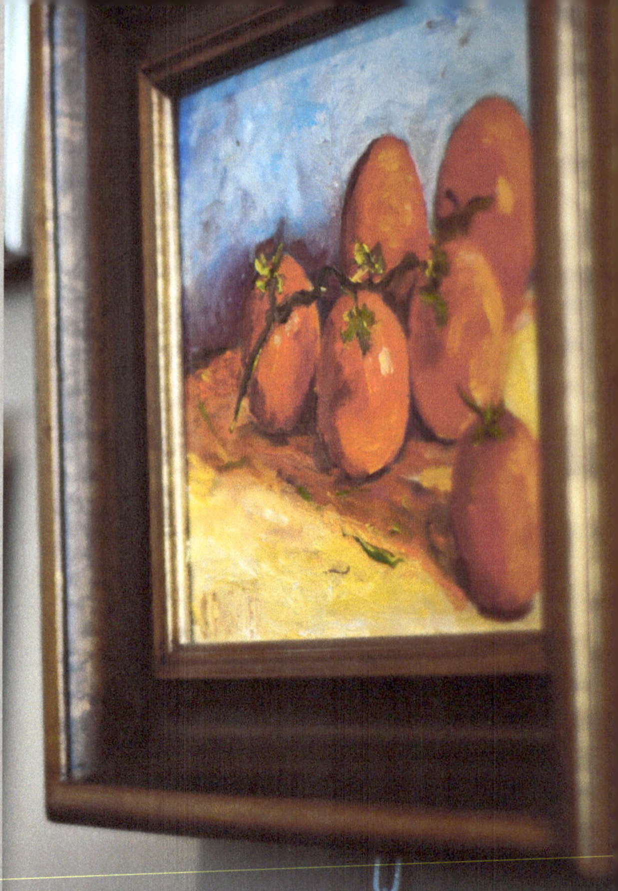

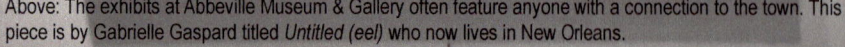

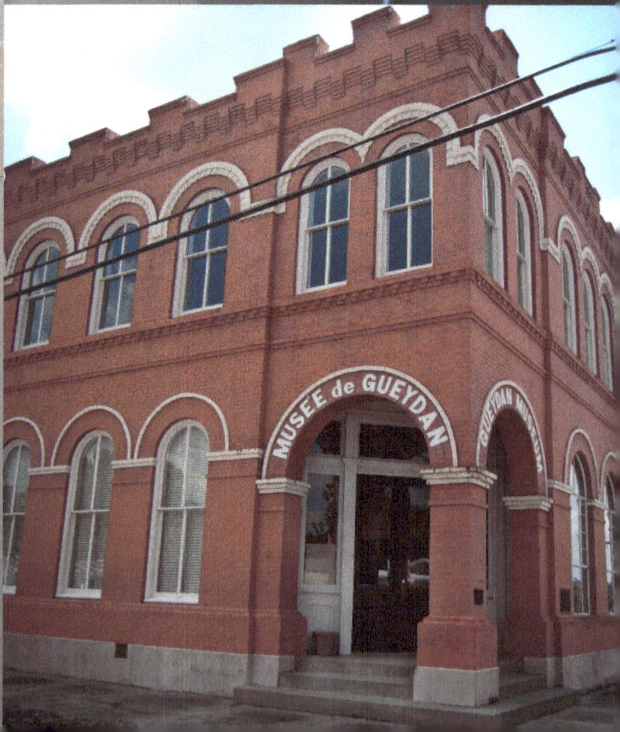

Above: The exhibits at Abbeville Museum & Gallery often feature anyone with a connection to the town. This piece is by Gabrielle Gaspard titled *Untitled (eel)* who now lives in New Orleans.

Right: Musée de Gueydan's local work ranges from still life to fine art to sculpture.

Abbeville Museum & Art Gallery

200 North Magdalen Square — Abbeville

The Vermilion Parish Veterans Memorial Building houses a conglomerate of organizations known as the Abbeville Cultural and Historical Alliance. That's where savvy Trailers will find the Abbeville Museum and Art Gallery. The group showcases a new exhibit each month and Curator Tony Mayard carefully chooses local artists and crafters who can provide something culturally new to the gallery. This gallery is certainly kid friendly with a section dedicated to children's exhibits.

Don't miss scenes depicting Abbeville's giant omelet celebration (the world's largest at the time) and rice mills that tell stories of the towns agricultural past. Lucky Trailers will catch the council's annual Carousel of Arts (happening every April) featuring live displays and performances celebrating the music, art, food, history, and culture of Vermilion Parish.

INSIDER'S TIP!

Call ahead to find out how you can participate in the Arts Council's sponsored art lessons and workshops for children.

Gueydan Museum

212 Main Street — Gueydan

You'll traverse rice fields and endless skies on your way to Gueydan, and it's worth every minute. The first thing you'll notice on arrival is a truly magnificent tree sculpture in the rear of the museum. Chainsaw Artist Burt Fleming sculpted this menagerie of a sun god, gators, bears and lions (oh my!).

The place is a tribute to Southern hospitality as you'll likely be offered cookies, coffee and plenty of welcoming conversation. Volunteers and Curator Jane Hair maintain rotating exhibits by local artists, many of which are for sale. You'll find great works from Theresa de Perrodil Trahan, Ann Ella Joubert, and Shirley Gauthier.

INSIDER'S TIP!

Ask about the albino nutria taxidermy in the rear. It defies description!

VIVIAN ALEXANDER STUDIO & GALLERY

6165 Picard Lane — Milton

The Vivian Alexander Studio and Gallery is a treasure that can only be found down long back roads and across cattle guards. Set deep within a field, surrounded by cattle, lies the gallery famous for gold and diamond encrusted eggs reminiscent of Russian legend.

Don't doubt your love for egg art — even if you don't think it's your thing. As Alex and his daughter guide you through this hidden sanctuary, you'll quickly realize how lucky you are to see their work. Their masterpieces have been created for movies like Warner Brother's "The Sitter" and advertising pieces for Smirnoff Vodka. The location and unique artwork makes this gallery a must-visit for all Art Trailers.

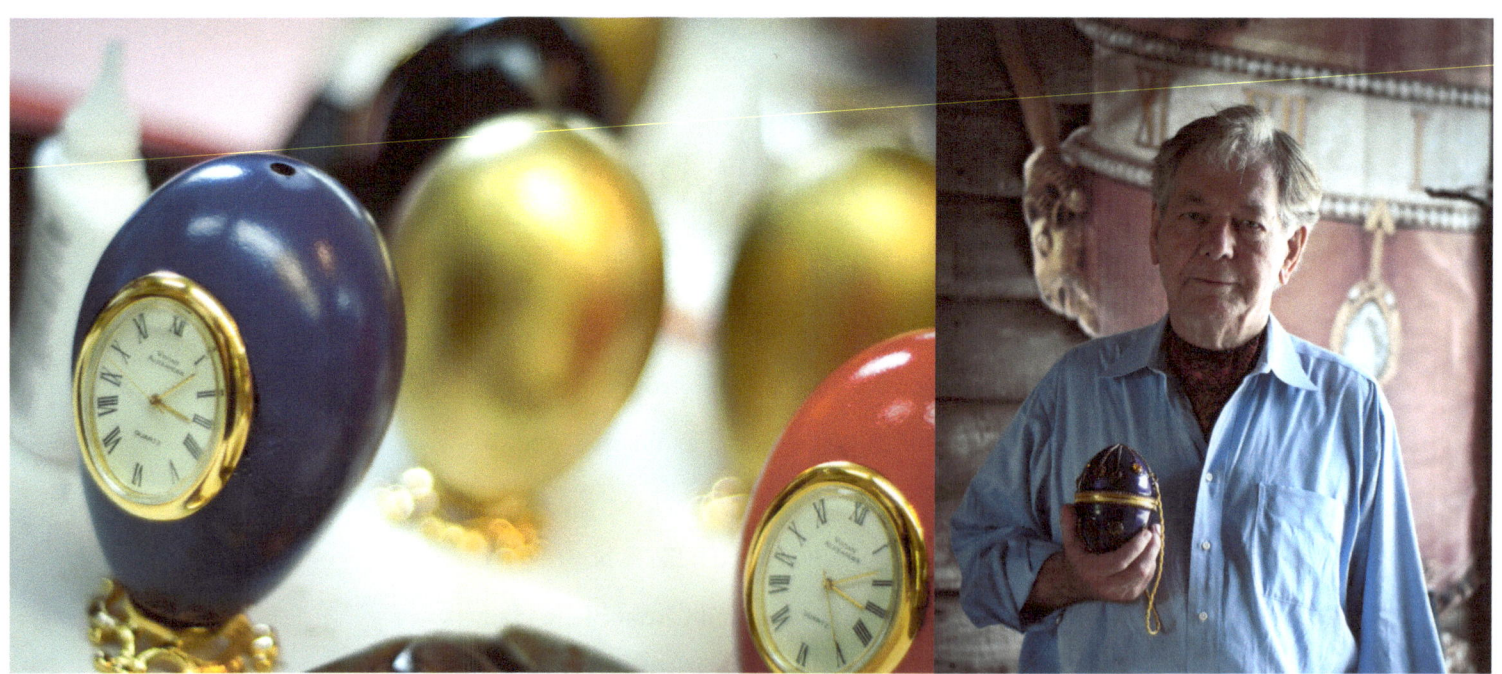

Above: Vivian Alexander is a working studio where you'll have ample opportunity to see the artists creating their signature pieces.

Right: The work continues the tradition of Fabergé, Russian jeweler to the tsars, known for their similarly elaborate jeweled eggs.

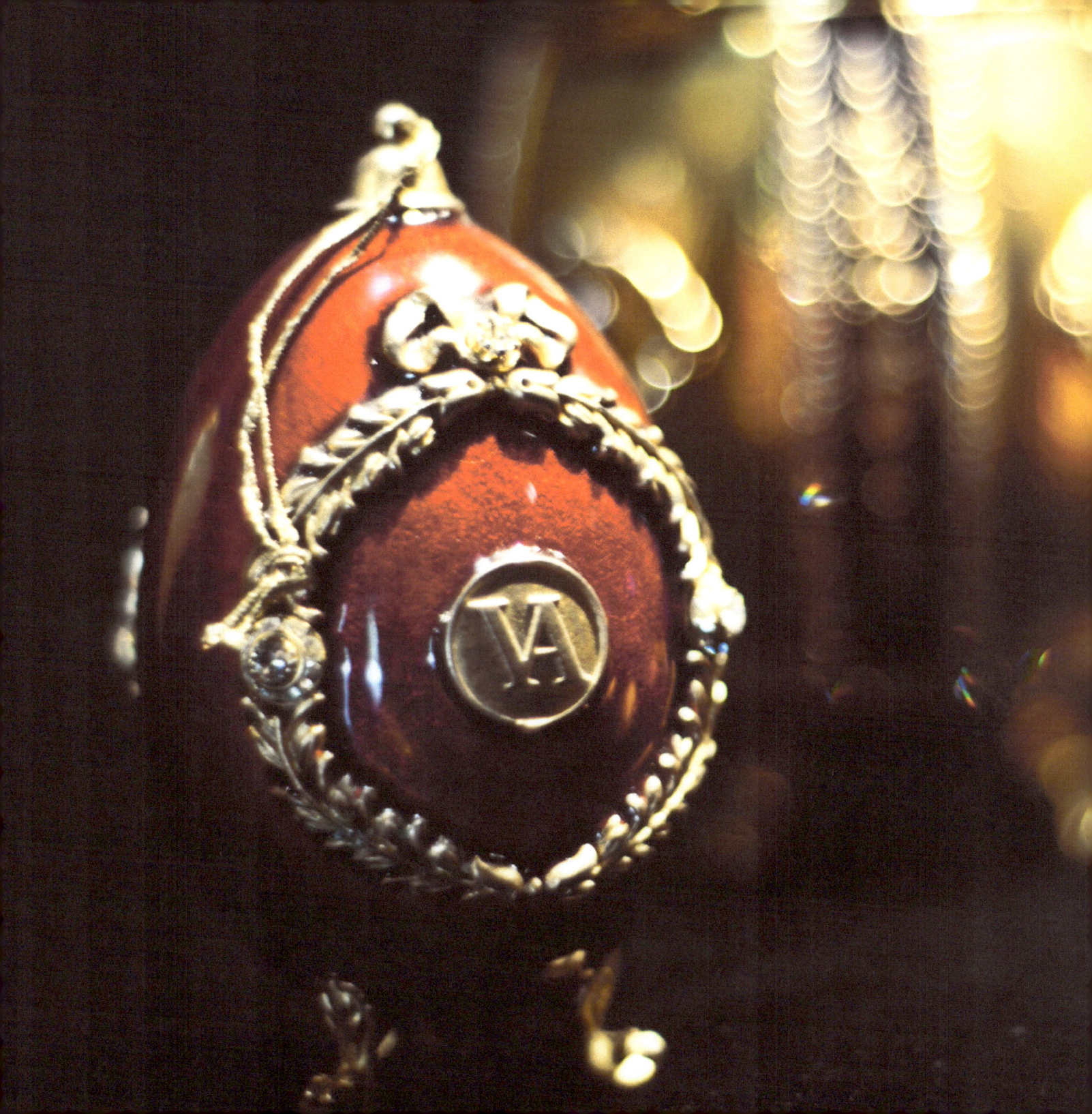

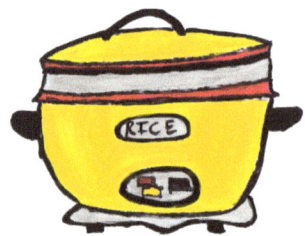

Acadia Trail

The railroad opened up commerce west of Lafayette and settlements soon followed. That's where we start the Acadia Trail, "Where the West Begins" in Scott. The land is broad and flat and filled with rice as we make our move into the dirt roads of Duson and later into Crowley, a hub of rice farming (residents there say "Life is rice and easy."). You'll follow Interstate 10 to the edge of Acadiana where the town of Jennings provides the final venue.

"From the native American Indians to the Cajun and Creole French, African American and the midwestern settlers brought in by the railroad industry, western Acadiana has a taste of everything. Aspects of all of these influences are evident in today's communities across the area and the blend has resulted in a pride and hospitality uniquely ours."

Another driving trail, Trail West is best visited Wednesday through Friday. You'll want to call ahead to Wortman Pottery as life on the family farm must be carefully intertwined with gallery visits.

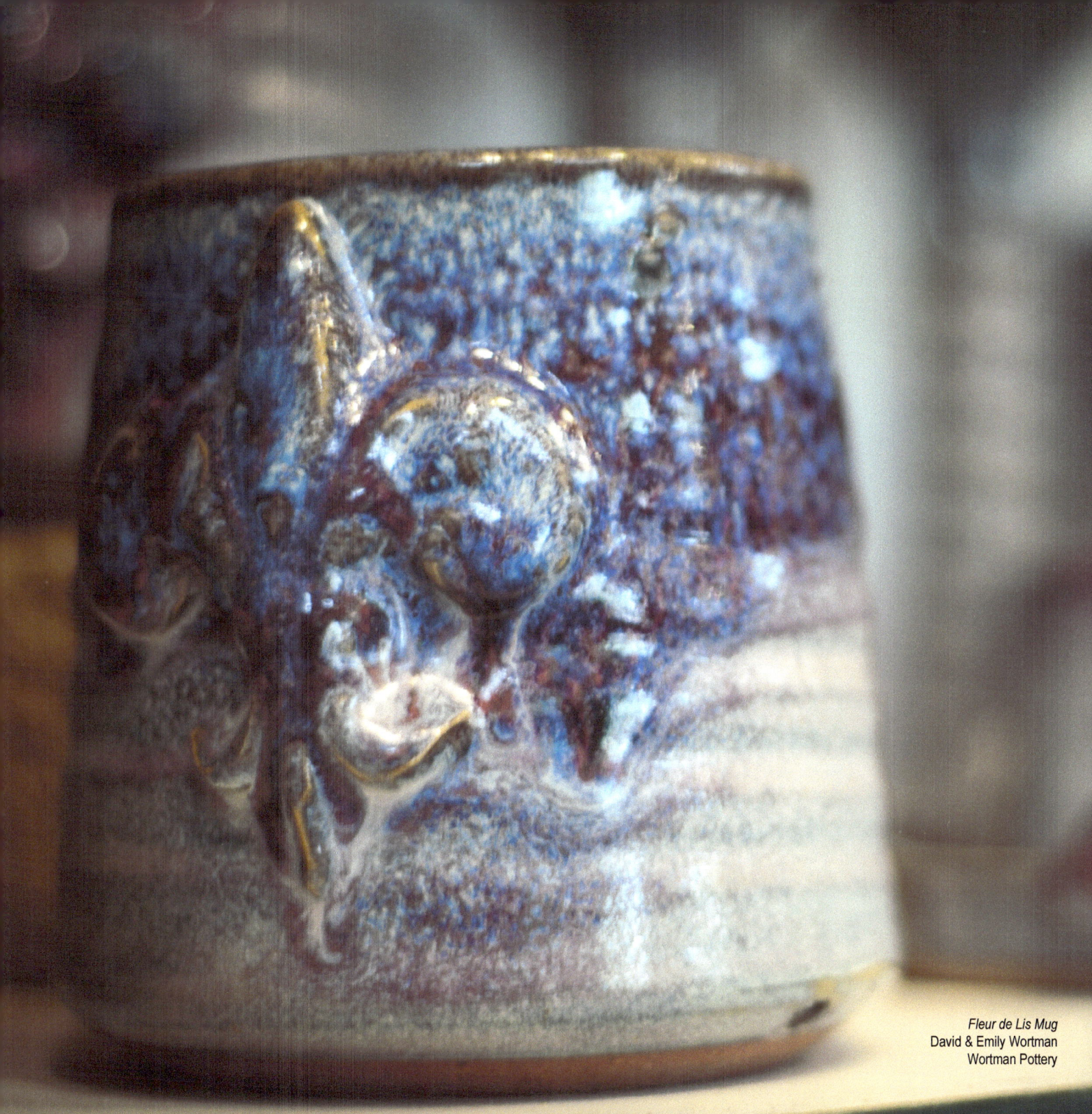

Fleur de Lis Mug
David & Emily Wortman
Wortman Pottery

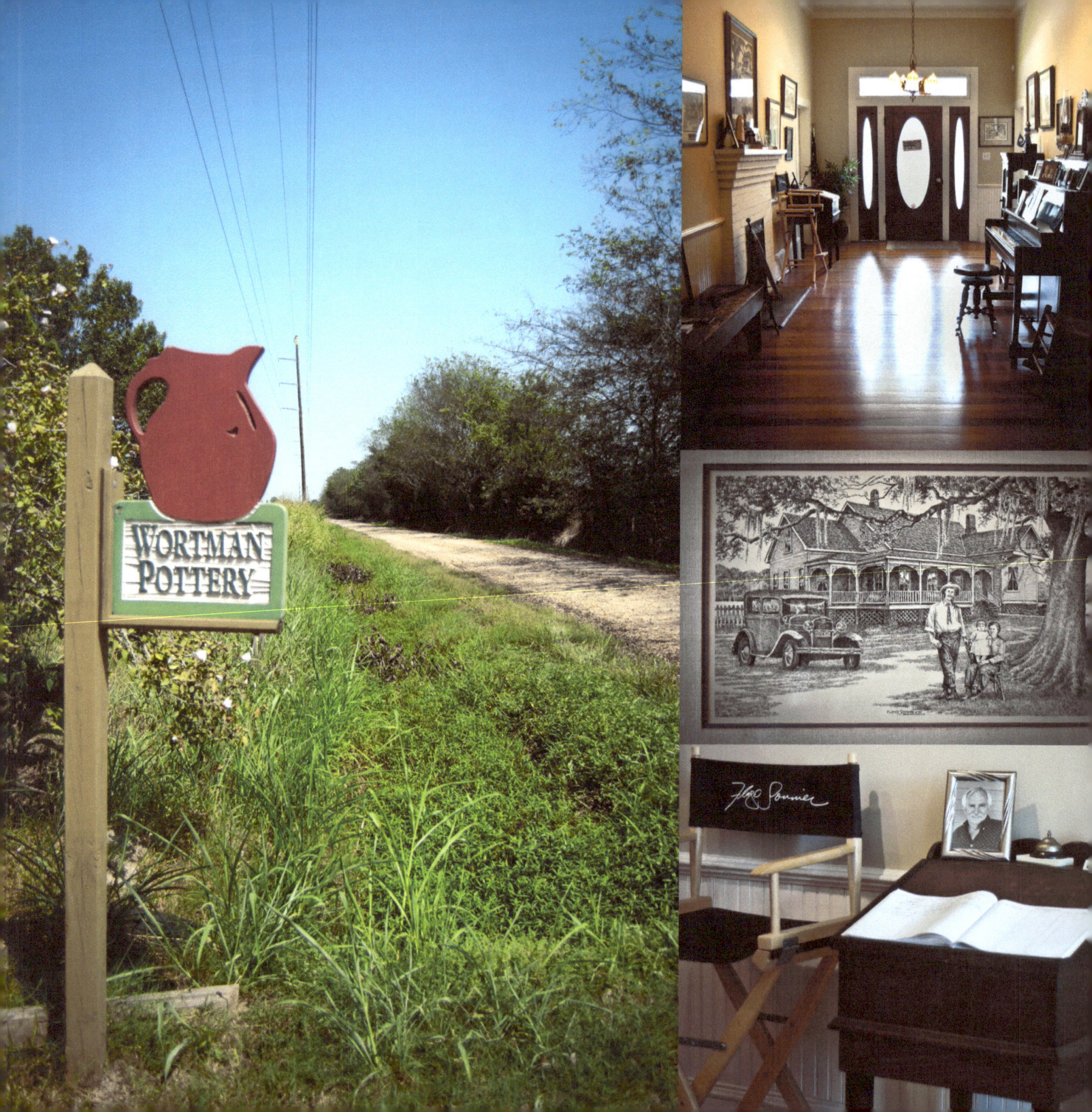

Beau Cajun Gallery

1010 St. Mary Street — Scott

Beau Cajun means Beautiful Cajun and provides a perfect description of work by Louisiana legend Floyd Sonnier. He got his start with charcoal drawings scratched from his father's iron kettle. From his childhood days on that sharecropper's farm, Sonnier dreamed of becoming a professional artist. He not only succeeded, he paved the way for other artist in our area to depict scenes of Cajun life.

Sonnier died in 2002 but his brilliant work still lives in the Beau Cajun, cared for lovingly by his wife Verlie. She'll tell you what she loves most about her husband's work is the way he drew from his heart. You'll see that heart and soul of Cajun life in each piece at this gallery, making this an historical and cultural must-see.

INSIDER'S TIP!

Beau Cajun Gallery not only offers Sonnier's original work for sale but also sells an array of Sonnier's re-printed work as gift items perfect for birthdays, holidays and "just because I love you" gifts for any art lover.

Wortman Pottery

1769 Potters Road — Duson

This is a true Art Trailer's adventure. The long gravel road calls you onward toward this nationally reputed working farm known as Wortman Pottery.

The family farm was established around 1890 and, since then, the Wortman's have found refuge in creating handcrafted, functional pottery designed to enrich daily life. You'll find dishes, oil candle holders, soap containers, mugs, platters, pitchers, bowls, trays and many other pieces in a range of beautiful blue hues. Ask for a tour of the studio to learn their unique process of pottery making.

INSIDER'S TIP

Wortman's is on a working farm, so call in advance to get the best experience.

Far Left: Wortman Pottery is truly a find. When you've located it, you'll feel a sense of adventure.

Left: Floyd Sonnier's work celebrates Cajun heritage. His studio is situated in the midst of the growing small town of Scott.

THE GALLERY

220 North Parkerson Avenue — Crowley

As you pull into a parking space in downtown Crowley, a giant mural confirms you've found The Gallery. Subsidized by the Crowley Art Association, this space features work from more than sixty-three local artists. You'll find pieces ranging from paintings to jewelry, photography to stained glass, even handmade clothing. It's a multifaceted feast for Trailers who enjoy a range of visual art.

INSIDER'S TIP

Visit the first Saturday of each month for one of the gallery's main attractions, a traditional gala celebration.

What also makes this gallery awesome is its raw brick walls that hold an authentic place for the local community to connect over any type of art. The learning environment gives way to the celebration of living that seems to thrive under this small roof. My experience here leaves an everlasting smile on my face as I watch the locals create their wonderland within The Gallery's walls.

ZIGLER MUSEUM

411 Clara Street — Jennings

My Art Trailer instincts don't often lead me to mainstream museums, but this one's an exception worth noting. Housed in a turn of the century mansion, the venue hides two additional gallery wings of painterly, realistic Southwestern Louisiana wildlife dioramas and fine art collections of European and American artists. The museum features some of the finest art in Southwest Louisiana and much of it is for sale. You'll have plenty of reasons to return as the central galleries feature rotating exhibits. All of the work here is truly poetic to say the least and you'll enjoy the organized flow that Zigler Museum has in store for you.

INSIDER'S TIP

Visit during holiday season for the Festival of Christmas, a display of elaborately decorated trees.

Top Right: The Gallery in Crowley holds an impressive range of local works and is bustling with activity on a regular basis.

Bottom Right: The Zigler Museum holds an extensive collection of art plus seasonal historical displays.

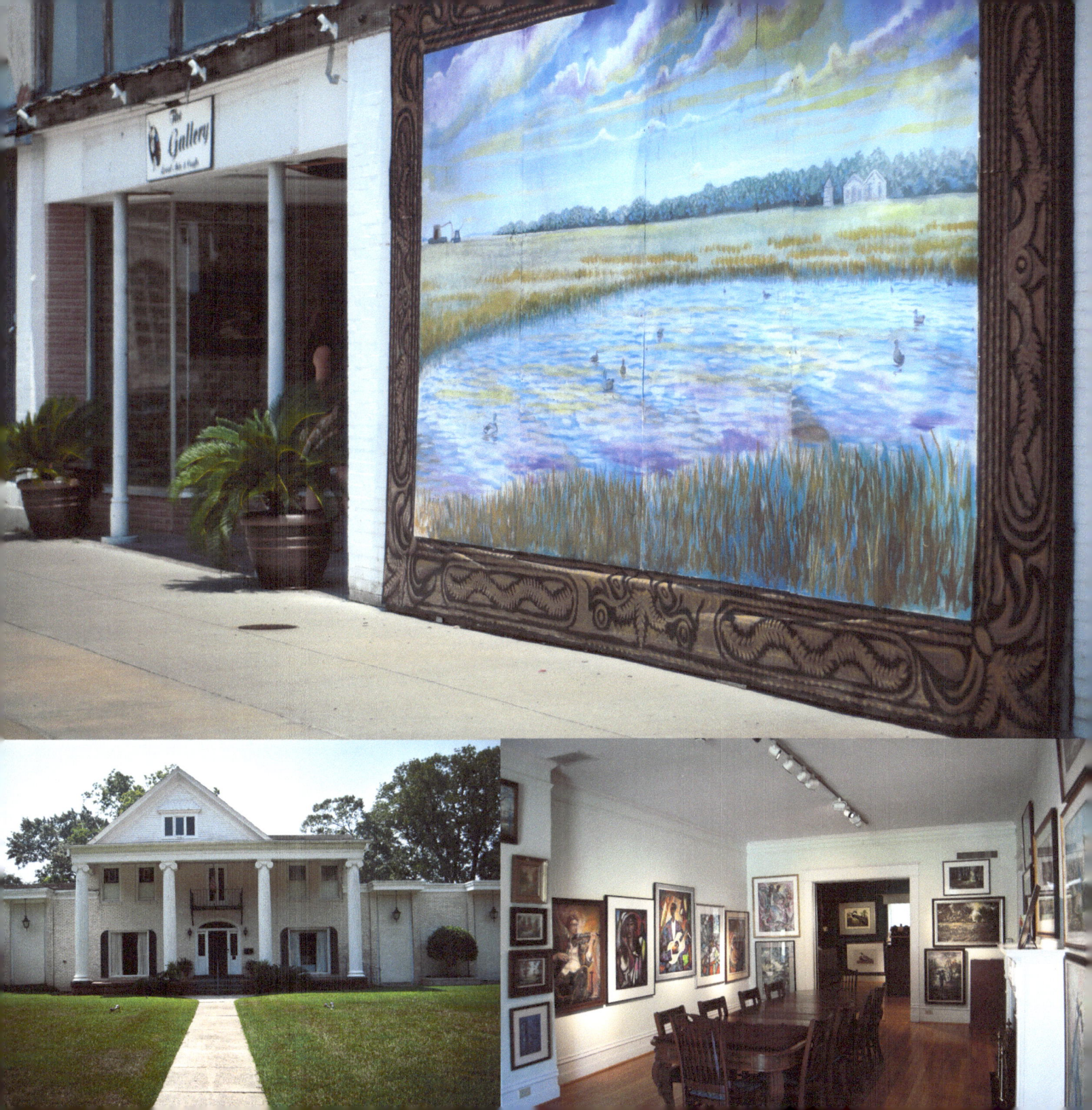

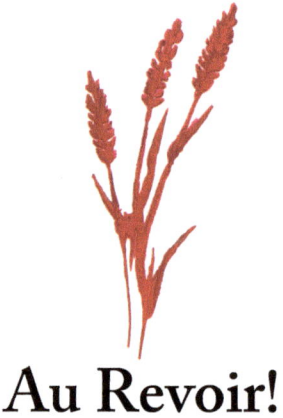

Au Revoir!

I hope you've enjoyed Trailing with me as this Acadiana Trail experience has brought me pure joy and inspired my passion for Acadiana's local art scene. We're fortunate to have so many local artists and venues wholeheartedly display their work for our delight. My wish is for you to relish in the paint and creativity.

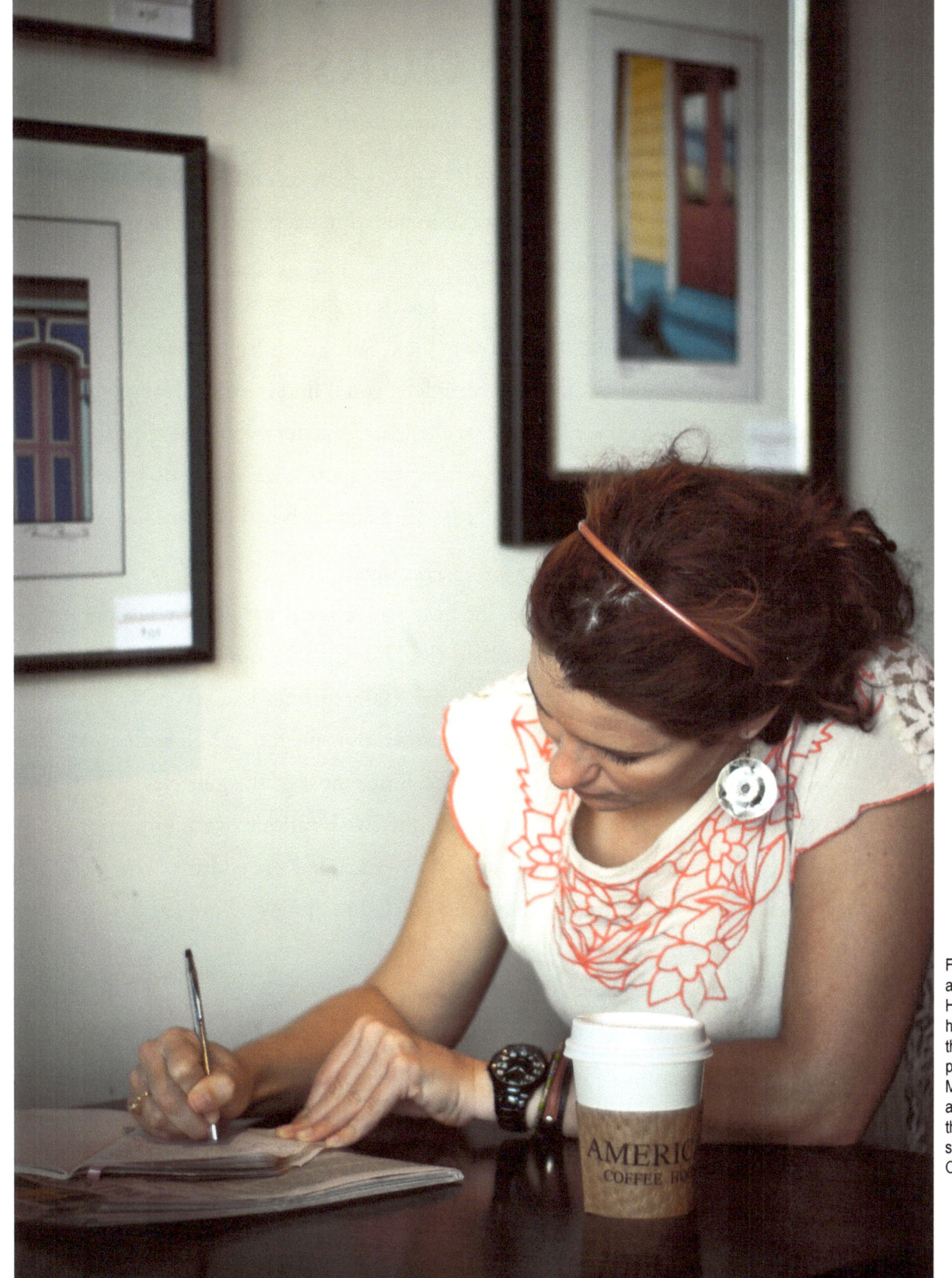

Foret writes notes at America's Coffee House. Behind her you can see the work of local photographer Maureen Dugas and her series on the architectural styles of New Orleans.

SEE FOR YOURSELF!

Tips for trips on The Acadiana Art Trail.

This art trail begs to be seen and it's easier than you might ever imagine. In addition to the insider's tips we've included in each trail, here are a few notes Art Trailers will appreciate.

Locals

If you live along the trail you're in luck. Since each leg of the trail is designed to take about a day to complete, you'll find it easy to complete all six over the course of several weekends. Consider overnight trips for the Lafayette and Teche trails — these two spots have lots to do within walking distance and the main cities are filled with bed & breakfasts.

Travelers

If you're not from Acadiana, the best way to see the trail is by setting up camp in Lafayette (it's not called the Hub City for nothing). The city has a full-service airport serviced by five major airlines and several major rental car firms, plus a newly-constructed downtown transportation hub with Amtrak, Greyhound and eco-friendly city buses. Since most of the galleries are downtown, we recommend staying at one of the two boutique overnight options: The Juliet Hotel or Buchanan Lofts. We've included the address with each Art Trail location, handy for getting quick directions on your GPS or smart phone.

Weather

South Louisiana's climate is subtropical so prepare for intense heat and humidity in the months of July and August. The remainder of the year, however, temperatures are generally mild and comfortable. Some of the best months to visit are October and April, when you'll also find several local festivals in full swing.

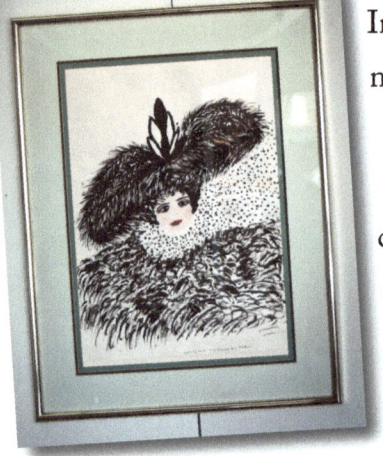

Untitled
Edesse Leger
The Gallery

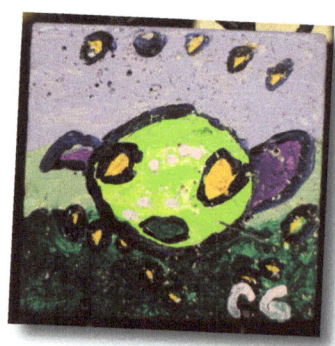

Under the Sea
Caroline G
St. Pierre's Center for the Arts

Food

For Cajuns, eating is practically a sport, so bring your appetite. Spring visitors can enjoy boiled crawfish, usually in season from January through Easter and a popular dish during Mardi Gras. Though served year round, dishes like gumbo and étouffée are popular during the fall when cooler weather inspires warmer menu items.

Lafayette's spring visitors might catch Festival International, the world's largest free Francophone festival. It's a great source for international music, cuisine and (of course) a bevy of local and international art.

Fall travelers can catch a range of festivals in a number of Acadiana Art Trail towns. October brings Festival Acadien et Creole, specifically designed to celebrate local art, music and cuisine.

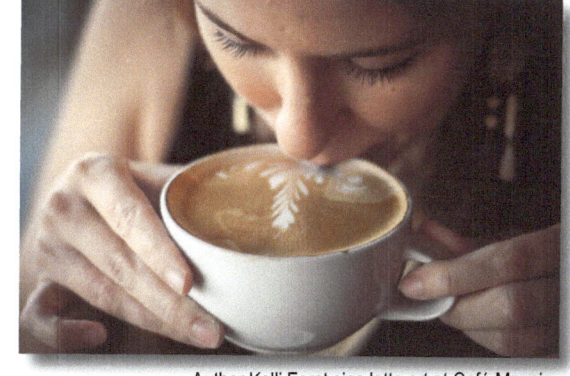

Author Kelli Foret sips latte art at Café Mosaic.

Travel Resources

These resources are filled with detailed information to help you plan your trip:

For hotels, trip planning, festival seasons and other attractions:

- **Acadia Parish Tourism Commission** — AcadiaTourism.org
- **Iberia Parish Convention & Visitors Bureau** — IberiaTravel.com
- **Lafayette Convention & Visitors Bureau** — LafayetteTravel.com
- **St. Landry Parish Visitors Center** — CajunTravel.com
- **St. Martin Parish Tourist Information** — CajunCountry.org
- **Vermilion Parish Tourist Commission** — Vermilion.org

For cultural stories and guides:

- **Local Artists and More Galleries** — ArtTrailLady.com
- **Local Restaurants** — EatLafayette.com
- **Love of All Things Southern** — DeepSouthMag.com

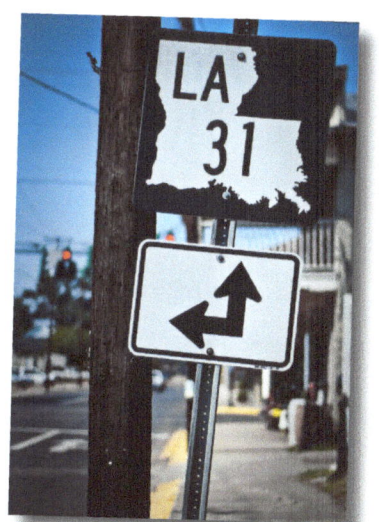

You'll quickly learn that some of Louisiana's most beautiful places lie along back roads.

THE ACADIANA ART✠TRAIL

THE ESSENTIAL GUIDE TO FINDING LOCAL ART IN CAJUN COUNTRY.

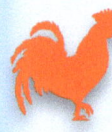
LAFAYETTE TRAIL
One of the best ways to maximize your local art experience is in the city of Lafayette, where you'll find eleven venues from ancient to modern, many within walking distance of each other.

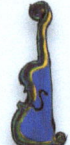
TECHE TRAIL
Another densely packed trail, the Teche Trail brings you through the heart of Breaux Bridge and ends in nearby St. Martinville. Bring your appetite, as many of the galleries double as eateries.

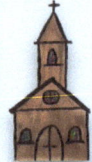
PRAIRIE TRAIL
It's easy to see the landscape change from slow rolling hills to prairies along the Prairie Trail. The trail's student art, stained glass and strange jewelry will delight you with the unexpected.

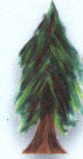
COTEAU TRAIL
The Coteau Trail guides you through some of Acadiana's newest, growing, hidden art communities. It's deceptively short, but you'll have plenty to see.

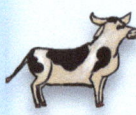
VERMILION TRAIL
The southern-most trail, the Vermilion Trail includes primitive, still life, folk art and surprise pieces in taxidermy and Russian-style eggs.

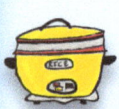
ACADIA TRAIL
Journey West through never-ending rice fields and a variety of pen and ink, pottery and paintings classic and modern.

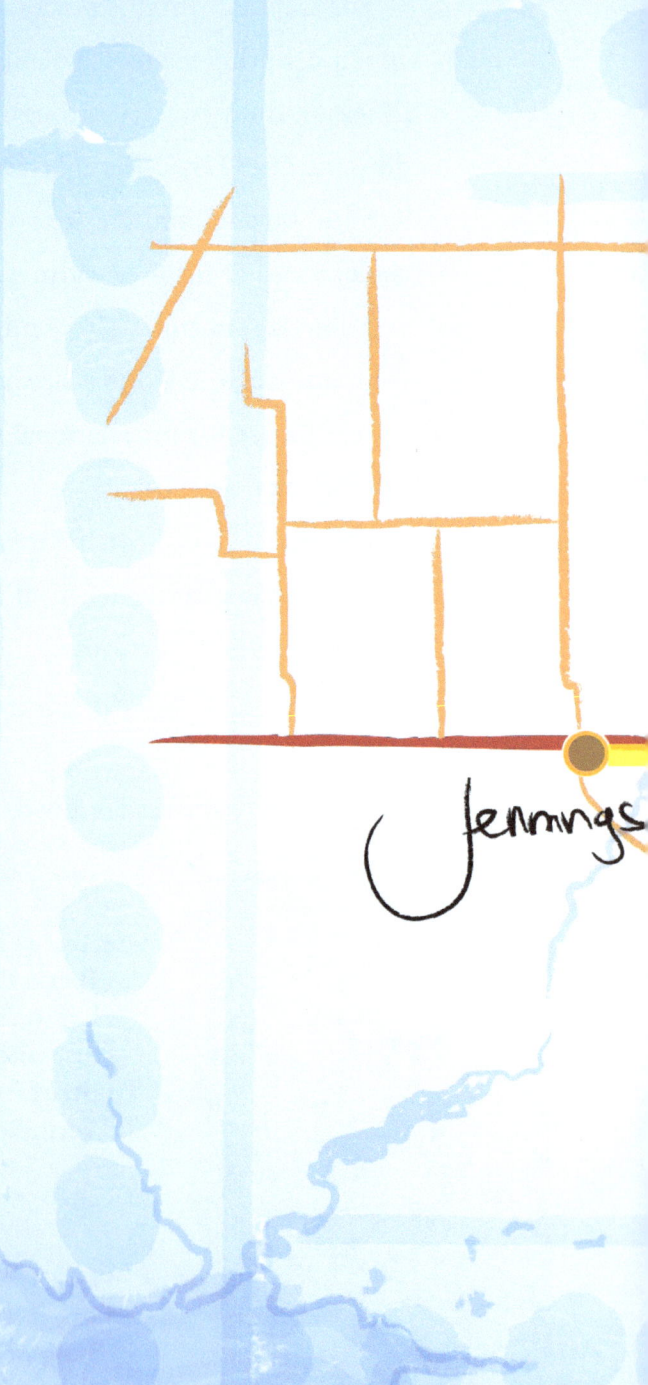
Jennings

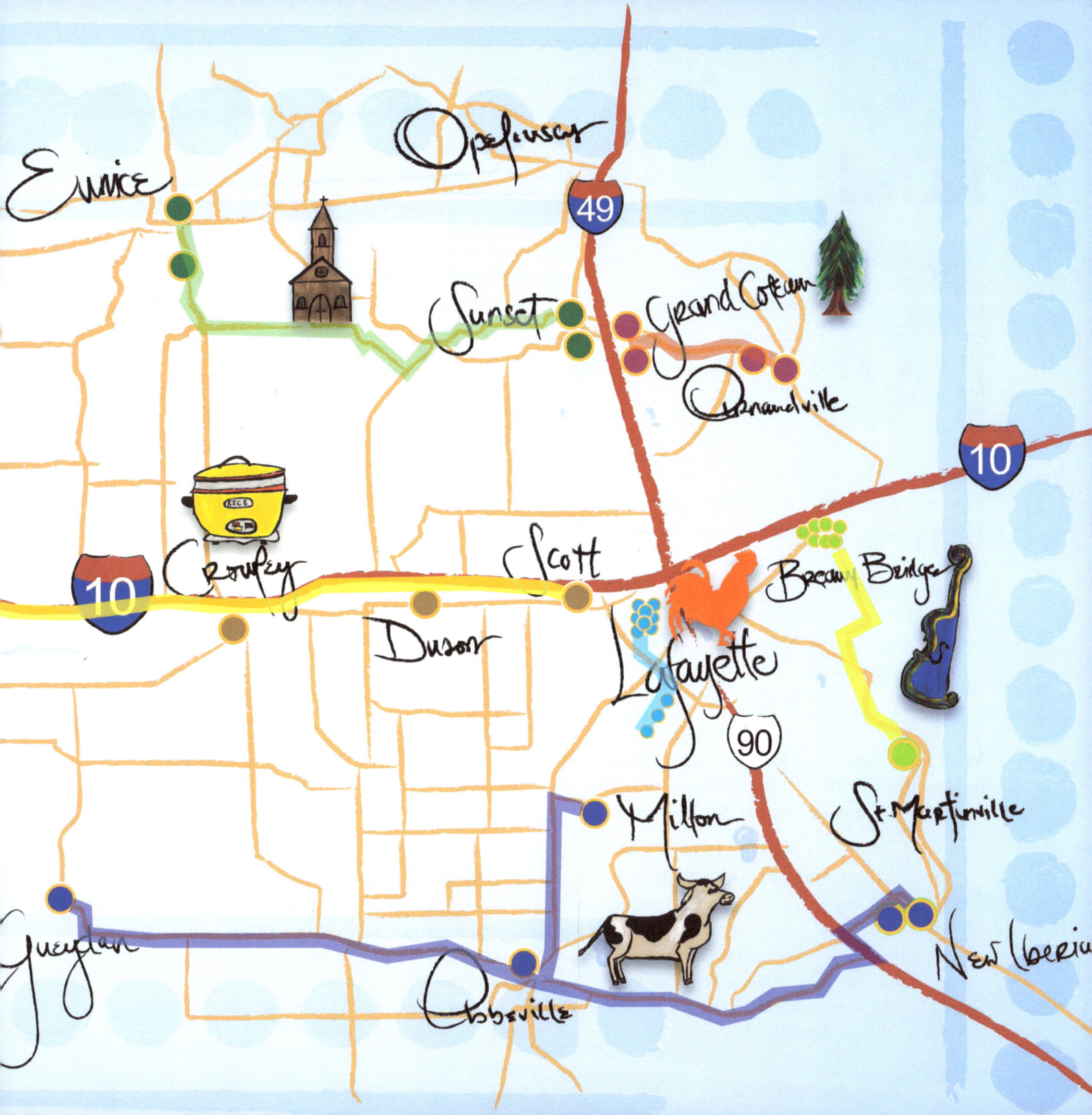

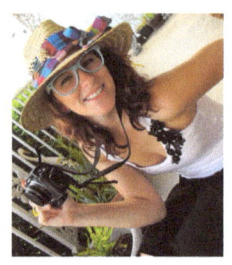

Kelli Foret's artistic influences are noticeably Cajun and deceptively deep. Her painted canvases, commonly made of sinker cypress (straight from the Atchafalaya Basin), reflect a range of primitive folk designs and hint at her international travels. Her photos make you smile. Her writing makes you fall in love with places you never heard of before. It's a visual-story-mix fitting any gumbo girl. *The Acadiana Art Trail* is her first book, but not her last. Follow her continuous art trail adventures at **ArtTrailLady.com**.

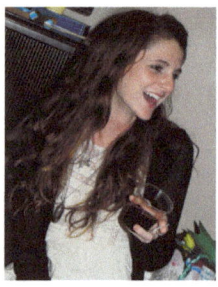

Lauren Hensgens earned her Bachelor of Fine Arts degree in Photography from the University of Louisiana. After her studies, she spent several years in Costa Rica shooting rainforests, wildlife and oceanscapes. Now back in Lafayette, Louisiana, she teaches art throughout the parish. See more of her work at **LaurenHensgens.com**.

Special thanks to the artists, gallery owners and tourism professionals who shared their work in this book. Painted icons are original works by Kelli Foret. The travel map was created by Angelina Leger. All photographs are by Lauren Hensgens except for the author's photo, which was taken by Maureen Dugas.

Back cover, clockwise from left: Tree sculpture at Musée Gueydan; "Cedric" by Amy Guidry at The Zigler Museum; Various landscapes by Donald LeBlanc at Gallery 549; Various gallery signs; "Have some coffee," with Ms. Jane Hair at Musée Gueydan; Stained glass by Craig McCullen at WhooJoo Gallery; "Louis Armstrong" by Adrian Fulton at Adrian Fulton Gallery.

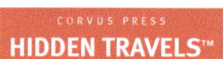

Want more books like this? The Hidden Travels series of books focuses on day trips to places less traveled and hidden finds usually reserved for locals. Why be a tourist when you can be a Hidden Traveler? Discover the hidden world around you at HiddenTravels.com.

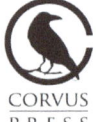